TABLE OF CONT

NOTES FOR A MAGAZINE

Sinister Wisdom 105: *Passion Fruit and Wet Flowers* is the summer issue of *Sinister Wisdom*'s forty-first year of publishing. What a journey it has been and what a future *Sinister Wisdom* has! Long-time readers know that the first issue of *Sinister Wisdom* published on July 4, 1976, the bicentennial anniversary of the United States. Forty-one years later, *Sinister Wisdom* publishes its 105th issue, continuing to celebrate revolutionary lesbian-feminist consciousness.

Sinister Wisdom 105: *Passion Fruit and Wet Flowers* includes the best creative writing by lesbians accepted during the past two years through our open submission process. *Sinister Wisdom* is always open to receive work and always reading work submitted by writers around the globe.

The creative work in *Sinister Wisdom* 105: *Passion Fruit and Wet Flowers* is an eclectic mix of poetry, fiction, a play, and creative non-fiction. Long-time readers of lesbian literature will recognize some of our contributors, including Minnie Bruce Pratt, Carla Tomaso, Yvonne Zipter, Cassandra Langer, Suzanne Gardinier, and Teresa Baum. New and emerging writers are in this issue as well, demonstrating the continued vibrancy of lesbian writers. I was particularly delighted to include work by María DeGuzmán, Arya F. Jenkins, Petra Kuppers, Cecilia Kiely, and Lauren Dunn in *Sinister Wisdom* 105: *Passion Fruit and Wet Flowers.* Though every single piece in this issue of Sinister Wisdom is a piece that I first fell in love with on the screen and am pleased to present to you now in printed form. I am grateful to Sara Gregory, a student at New College Florida who interned this spring semester with *Sinister Wisdom* and was integral to the curation and completion of this issue.

You may notice your packets of *Sinister Wisdom* getting a little thicker. In addition to mailing you the quarterly copy of the journal, we have been tucking in little surprises to reflect the current political moments in which we live. In the spring issue (*Sinister Wisdom* 104: *Lesbianima Rising*), you found a large postcard with an etching by lesbian artist Minnie Chiu on one side and a poem by lesbian poet Cheryl Clarke on the other side. Both of these pieces responded to the feminist March in Washington the day after the 2017 inauguration.

In this issue of *Sinister Wisdom*, you will find a similar insert with a selection reprinted from the first year of *Sinister Wisdom*'s publishing in 1976/1977 and a response piece by Shawn(ta) Smith-Cruz. This insert is part of a new annual series, *Anticipating Sinister Wisdom's Croning*, leading up to *Sinister Wisdom*'s fiftieth anniversary in 2026. Each year, I will ask a contemporary artist to review a year of issues from the first ten years of *Sinister Wisdom*, select something to reprint, and write a creative, contemporary response to the original piece. I am thrilled Shawn agreed to inaugurate this ten-part series. I hope you will collect all of the inserts in the series as a part of the delight and anticipation of the golden anniversary of *Sinister Wisdom*.

This new golden anniversary project is made possible by support from generous donors and friends of *Sinister Wisdom*. Thank you to everyone who supports the journal and helps us reach new audiences to nurture and support lesbian art and literature and lesbian creativity.

In sisterhood,

Julie R Enszer
July 2017

THE TATTERED BLANKET

Pat Spears

N ow that I'm alone, my concentration lapses, and when I see Josey standing at the end of the lane, waiting as we agreed, I brake hard, sending the truck's bald tires sliding to a jerky stop twenty yards beyond her. I watch her approach in the side mirror, and she's frowning. Maybe she, too, worries that I've slipped a cog or two. She opens the door, gets in, and her young face reshapes itself into a sly, playful smile.

"Damn, old woman, you trying to outrun one of Khrushchev's Cuban missiles?" She means to rub off my embarrassment, pretending a nervous glance into an October sky the color of faded denim.

"Huh, never mind any missile. That shit there is bound to kill us before the Russians." I nod in the direction of a grey cloud of chemical exhaust rising and drifting westward from the stacks of the local pulp wood mill, its putrid odor of rotten eggs and pine rosin fouling the air.

"Pour me another while you're at it." I hand her the battered thermos, a veteran of many nameless journeys, and she pours expertly to the cup's circled stain; the rough road mark. The strong scent of chicory and bourbon fills the cab.

I flip the truck around in the road and drive back in the direction I came. Josey settles onto the tattered wool blanket covering the ripped seat, her hands wedged under her bare thighs.

"This itchy old rag's like sitting in a patch of sandspurs. Beats me why you go on treating it like a faithful dog. It's got to be older than me."

"Never you mind, girlie. That blanket's one hundred percent my business." The first time I called her "girlie" she was eleven or twelve. She let me know in no uncertain terms that "girlie" was for sissies, and she for sure wasn't one.

I've held on to the blanket for nearly two decades, and from time to time I do rethink why. My pointless exercise always comes down to the fact that I remain royally pissed. Ruth always said my anger would make me an early corpse. Then God's revenge works in mysterious ways.

At the Jameson-Lake Wilmoco crossroads I turn eastward, and the clatter of the truck panics a flock of sparrows. The tiny birds lift in a single frantic motion from the wet, grassy shoulder of the road and fly away in a tight formation. Ruth spoke of quails scattering widely when threatened, in the hope that at least a few survived. I've come to know that surviving is a damn hard way to go.

Josey steals glances, the puffiness under her dark eyes evidence that sleep was a stranger to both of us. I think she must study my intent. I'd asked only for her company, and had said nothing as to why.

I tell her there's ham and biscuits with Ruth's blackberry jam in the brown bag on the seat next to her. She bites into the warm biscuit, jam oozing from its crispy edges, and she licks it away. As a child, she'd regularly shown up at suppertime, so much so that Ruth routinely set a place for her. Those times when she failed to show or ran late, Ruth and I ate in comparative silence, each listening for her hurried footsteps approaching, the certainty of the slamming door, and Josey bursting into the kitchen, breathless and apologetic, taking a quick seat at the table. While I grumbled that my food was stone cold, thanks to her, Ruth gently reminded her that, late or not, dirty hands were not welcome at our table. The child possessed a gift for holding onto to dirt as if it were a family heirloom.

Josey stuffs the last of the biscuit in her mouth and speaks around her food. "You remember when we'd considered ourselves burning good daylight if we weren't on the river before now?" She exhales sharply, her words rushed, and she probes the familiar for the ease we once shared like the very air we breathed.

"We'd have our hooks baited, lines dropped into the fishiest spots, corks sitting at full attention, and our mouths set just so," I respond.

"And I'd pray the bigger fish took my bait first." Her tone shifts, no longer playful. "It was you who taught me not to waste my prayers on things beyond God's concern." She stares ahead through the windshield, her mouth set hard against all she's learned, and although I've spit in the face of *His* arbitrariness my entire life, her bitterness is her own.

I steer the truck onto Old Church Road, and ahead the simple, lapped cypress church stands mid-point on a slight rise in an otherwise flat terrain. The steeple holds no bell to summon its faithful, and its rough spire made of shaved pine saplings speaks to the long-standing impoverishment of its congregation.

I park the truck beneath the spreading branches of an ancient live oak, drain the last of the cold coffee, and step out of the truck. Josey follows me, and although she must now think she knows why I've brought her here, she still doesn't ask.

Angie Otterman approaches on stiff, arthritic knees along a worn trail that runs between her family's failed farm and the church grounds. Angie's stomach and breasts sag under the coarse cotton print dress sown from feed bags. Her sap long ago spent on a two-year birth cycle that produced ten living children; the last two full-term little boys were stillborns. While fully accepting her fate of eternal damnation, she sought my help for her pregnant fourteen-year-old daughter. At no time did she speak of the circumstances surrounding the child's pregnancy. Then, I required no explanation. When I'd done what she came for, she paid with two settings of fertile eggs and walked dry-eyed off my porch, her arm cradling her weeping daughter.

"Morning, Miss Mattie. Is it our Savior Jesus Christ who brings you to His Father's house?" She smiles, her devotion absolute, and in my arrogance I pity her, while admiring the tenacity of her simple faith. She clutches a fist of freshly picked wildflowers intended for the church altar.

"Not today, Angie. It would appear I'm good for a while longer on my own."

Her brow gathers, but her concern is no longer with what she must think of as my blasphemy. Rather, she cowers at the approach of her husband, Jacob, a brutal, heartless man I've come to despise. I've treated Angie and their children for concussions, fractures, lacerations, bruises, and crushed spirits more times than I want to remember. He glares at Angie, his hard eyes burning with reprisal, and she stands slumped, eyes downcast. He doesn't as much as look at Josey or me but walks on toward the church, entering through its narrowest of doors.

"Forgive my husband. He doesn't require love. Only obedience." She steps closer and, her voice strong, says, "I know our sweet Miss Ruth favored her roses. Just the same, I think she'd like these pretties." She hands me the bouquet of wildflowers, turns and follows her husband into the church.

I turn to Josey who has continued to stand near the truck. Her expression is one of empathy, and I reach my hand to her, and hers is moist inside mine. We walk beneath a rusted metal archway, three rotund cherubs poised atop, each grasping harps in their plump hands. Morning dew beads like teardrops on the sweet-smelling honeysuckle vine that entwines the arch, and sunlight turns each droplet into a prism of rainbow colors.

We walk among row after row of graves with tombstones of porous lime rock, blackened with age. Bread loaf-shaped indentations in the coarse sand are marked with simple, decaying wooden crosses or by weathered cards slipped inside clear plastic holders, fastened to metal stakes tapped into the ground. All bear the Irish, Scottish, German, and English names of the town's pioneer families: human chains stretching back six generations, buried so close I imagine their bones rubbing together on windy nights.

I stop at the newly erected double gravestone cut from solid granite, its silver-gray face polished to a smooth brilliance, bearing the inscription:

RUTH ANN O'RILEY
BELOVED COMPANION OF MARGARET E. FRANKLIN
BORN OCTOBER 5, 1909 — DIED JANUARY 9, 1961
MARGARET E. FRANKLIN
BELOVED COMPANION OF RUTH ANN O'RILEY
BORN MAY 16, 1907— DIED

Josey's hand flies to her mouth, her fingertips pressed to her lips, and she whispers, "Oh, damn, Mattie. It ... it's everything." Her tears erupt as she wraps her arms tightly about her chest and sways in rhythm with her grief.

"Yes, it is. Isn't it?" I kneel, place the wildflowers on the grave, and with a fingertip, I trace the truth of our love. The three decade-long life we shared is no longer a whisper between lovers, but a shout, chiseled into the granite for eternity. My fears melt, and my resolve flows through my veins as strong and warm as my very blood.

Josey swallows hard, struggling to speak, and when she does, her voice is hoarse, barely more than a whisper. "Mattie, I'm so ashamed. I should have been here with you, the way you and Miss Ruth were for me growing up." Her grief is so palpable it wears on my lingering resentment.

"Aw, child, burying our Ruth was the easy part. It's been the living afterward that's nearly killed me." I don't tell her that I still make coffee for two. That my recurring bouts of paralyzing despair result in me going weeks without refilling Ruth's hummingbird feeders. I try, but fail miserably with her roses; canes yield buds that refuse to open, bowing their heads, they turn brown, decay, and drop onto the ground. Then I've never had her ways with sustaining life. I don't admit to sitting alone far too many evenings on our back porch, drinking whiskey for the numbness it affords. Rather, I decide to tell her a different story.

"When those undertaker boys took her away, I couldn't bear being alone in our little house. So, I sat in my truck till Jake came with a bottle. We kept right on sitting and drinking until I felt I could face the truth, and he drove me to the funeral home. Dick Dawkins tried turning me away in favor of getting in touch with her nearest kin. Claimed the law was on his side. Like the law or that little shit had a side. Through my wrangling with Dawkins, Jake never uttered a word. Then all of a sudden, he grabbed that fat boy by the collar, hauled him into the back room, and flipped him butthole-upward onto a gurney. And in a calm voice, he threatened to pump him full of embalming fluid and to hand me a lighted cigarette. Needless to say, Mister-go-by-the-book got busy making arrangements, right down to roses or gladiolas."

Josey glances about the cemetery as though questioning such a story told among the dead, but in spite of her misgivings, our laughter surely turns heads among those in the church. I open my arms to her and our embrace momentarily pushes our separate losses aside, making our grief bearable.

We walk back along the path to where we left the truck, and Josey looks toward the church as an off-key rendition of *Onward Christian Soldiers* rises from the congregation and echoes across the clearing.

"Do you think Miss Ruth's safe here?"

I understand she wishes to be reassured that hatred and its violence stops with the grave, but I can't do that. I do tell her that men, women, and children openly wept at her funeral, while not one spoke our names in the same breath. Still I choose to set aside the evil I saw in the eyes of Jacob Otterman and accept that a gift of simple wildflowers is an act of compassion.

Reaching the crossroads, I pull the truck to a full stop and look in both directions, behavior that has nothing to do with a sudden inclination for the rules of the road. I look at Josey and her dark eyes hold words yet unspoken.

"What'd you say to our riding over to the beach? Checking out our old haunts? Maybe catch us a mess of soft-shells. Build a fire and stay over."

"The way we did when Jake came along and Miss Ruth made the best picnics ever?" She smiles, but it's her loneliness I know so well that squeezes my heart with love.

I pull the truck to a stop at Jake's filling station and direct Josey to retrieve the key from behind the kerosene tank and pump gas while I plunder the shed for the old crab nets and buckets Jake hung there for just such occasions. The nets are nearly rotted with age, but good for one last trip.

I pass the beer bucket containing four cold beers borrowed from the rusted cooler in the shed. Josey sets the bucket on the floorboard between her feet and locates the church key from the glove compartment, opening a couple. By the time we reach the beach, we've finished the beers.

I pull over at a boarded up Gulf station, tell Josey to wait, and walk around behind the building as if intent on peeing in the over-grown weeds. I rap on the barred door, tell the boy what I want, and he explains the three percent service charge. In less than five minutes I return with a five-pound chunk of ice in a croaker sack holding sliced bologna, chicken necks, beer, and RC colas with Wonder bread and Jack's assorted cookies in a brown bag.

"That's not exactly keeping the Sabbath, now is it?" Josey grins, placing the sack on the floorboard.

"If you know where to look, sin's for sale any day of the week. Otherwise it *is* a blue Sunday."

I park the truck on the edge of an oyster shell road, careful to keep the passenger side wheels out of a sand bog. Josey grabs up the sack, buckets, and nets, leaving me the brown bag, cooking pot from behind the seat, and the blanket. We trudge a quarter of a mile through palmetto clumps and twisted scrub oaks to a secluded strip of white sand lying between a high-tide lagoon and the blue-green waters of the bay.

On the shore's edge, a flock of pissed seagulls rise from the surf, flapping their noisy retreat. Ahead, the prevailing wind catches the heavy exhaust from the pulp mill, pushing its stench across the bay, sparing us the worst. I point out a shortleaf pine, its growth stunted, branches gnarled by constant salt spray and gulf wind. Perched on a lower limb, an anhinga spreads her bluish-black wings to dry, and beyond, in the lagoon, the silver backs of mullet flash in the sunlight. I draw in the salty air, embracing it in the way of a returning lover.

I squint across the wide expanse of water and I hear Ruth's excited voice, forever the teacher, speaking of the wide continental shelf, inviting a young Josey and Jake to imagine the shelf righting itself in some geological event, land pushing up out of the Gulf, and our standing in what would become the center of the state. Then there's no place or joy where loneliness does not dwell.

We slip off our shoes, roll up our pant legs, and wade into the foaming surf. We toss chicken necks, secured to lines, into the surf, baiting crabs, the midday sun warming our backs. Josey pulls her shirt over her head and ties it around her waist. Our pursuit takes us several miles along the narrow strip of sand, and we're alone for as far as I can see in any direction. When the bucket is filled with crabs, we walk back to where we stashed the food and drink.

Sitting on the sand beneath the rustle of a cabbage palm, I make fold-overs from the bologna and bread, and we polish off the last of the beers. When we've had our fill, I slip off behind a clump of palmetto and squat to pee. Josey packs away the remaining food and drink. I return and spread the army blanket, settling onto the warm sand for a nap.

Josey strips naked and wades into the surf. She's a big girl, her body muscled, her breasts firm, the circle around her nipples brown as tree ripened figs. Her strokes are strong and even; a young woman at ease in the water. She swims seventy yards or more to the edge of blue water, flips onto her back, and waves while bobbing like a fisherman's cork. Pushing her limit, she swims further, and I can no longer make her out, but I don't need to see to know the daring gleam in her eyes; her need for recklessness.

Josey walks out of the surf and when she's struggled into her cut-off jeans and tee shirt, she stands, looking out across the blue-green expanse to where water and sky become one, and she smiles. A memory or thought she doesn't share and maybe it's the gentle lapping of the waves spilling onto the sand that adds to what I sense as her new calm.

She comes to sit with me on the blanket, and she surprises me with, "How'd you know Miss Ruth was the love you could trust."

Love remains a mystery to me, and what little I do know of it defies the shape of words. Still, I tell Josey a parable.

"I remembered watching my grandpa work iron. He never hurried. Heated and cooled the iron, content to pound it into shape a little at a time, believing a good piece of iron would need shaping and reshaping with considerable care if it was to hold its core strength. Don't know if he was right or not, but I took his point."

"For a moment back there with Miss Ruth, I thought I knew all I needed to know. But now, I'm not as sure." She pauses, looks to a wider world she knows to distrust, and speaks not to me, but to that realization. "There's a woman I think I loved, but I let her get away without ever telling her as much."

"Ah, and who was it you didn't trust?"

She looks at me with the same bewilderment Ruth must have seen on my face in the moment my cowardice had nearly cost me her love: *Freedom, my love,* a naïve Ruth whispered, and even now I feel the sensation of her, nibbling my ear in the way that could make me purr. *Forevermore in the company of other women loving women. No need for lies. Our love free to bloom like wildflowers in a field, rooting out evil until there is no place for hatred to grow.* Her wonderfully alive face had brightened with such a dreamy smile. I'd scoffed, *Maybe Mars, but not here on Earth. Not in our lifetime.* She'd bolted out of bed, accusing me of always spoiling everything. I believe, even now, that she'd fully intended on staying away.

"Why didn't you tell me about you and Miss Ruth? It wasn't that much of a secret. I think I knew even before I knew about myself."

"What could I have told you that would have changed anything? Would you have left here understanding that we're no different? We laugh, cry, destroy, comfort, flirt, love, fuck, break hearts, and plot revenge. And if that elusive bitch, Lady Luck, smiles on us, we find a woman, pair up, lay claim, and hold on for dear life. Then I've left out the part where some of us get killed for doing as much."

She nods. "Still, I think I would've liked knowing I wasn't alone."

I give her that. But if it's platitudes she now wants, about the magic of finding a love that can save her, make all the risk worthwhile, I won't lie. I went after Ruth, not believing that her love, or the love of any woman, could save me, but I did believe loving her was reason enough for me to try saving my own troubled soul.

We gather the driftwood, downed palm fronds, and pine cones we'll need, and when the sun teeters on the razor-thin edge of the horizon, she builds a fire and I prepare the crabs. Filling the cook pot with salt water, I place the crabs on the wire mesh. When they have streamed, we sit back on the blanket and pick sweet meat from the shells, washing our food down with tepid RC Colas.

Josey adds the remaining twigs and palm branches and the flames flicker, catching hold, and we draw nearer to the fire's primordial powers to comfort. Josey stares into the darkness beyond the fire's light and asks, "What's to be done about the tombstone ... your half, I mean?"

"Uh, that," I pause, settling yet again to the inevitability of my own death. "Jake hasn't seen it yet. But whatever he feels, he'll do what's needed when the time comes."

What that sweet boy knows and has denied about Ruth and me could fill one of those poetry books he keeps hidden behind the seat of his truck, secretly reading as if Ruth's encouraging words still ring in his ears. He's read more than the lifetime total of all those whose old vehicles he labors to keep on the roads.

"Why him?" Her sense of betrayal is more real than I think she means to expose.

"He'll stay and you won't." I smile, wanting her to know that her leaving can be a good thing.

Her facial muscles relax as she slowly nods, and she's made a decision, requiring that my sadness give ground to her loneliness. Now I believe she knows why she leaves, and the harder part of knowing what of herself she'll need to leave behind when she goes.

We sit, neither talking, as the flames die, black-velvet darkness folding in around us. I think about how little I've taken from my own hard living, and decide to tell her the story of the blanket.

"After the war, a bunch of us queers got booted out of the service. Army paid shrinks to say we were crazy. We were all scared, some enough to tattle, thinking to save their own hides. Military handed out dishonorable discharges as freely as they had additive cigarettes. This old blanket became a daily reminder that nobody stood up for us. Not even those whose lives we'd saved."

I don't tell her that parades and celebrations had popped up in every little chicken-shit town across the country, and I was a proud soldier. I wanted to wear my uniform and march in just one of those home-grown parades. Ruth threw me a private homecoming celebration and I dressed in my uniform, stripped of its insignia and medals. But Ruth was not to be outdone: she pinned construction paper medals on my jacket, escorted me to a candlelight dinner in our own tiny kitchen, and afterwards, we danced until two in the morning to Benny Goodman's band.

For the second time today, I taste salt on my lips, and I decide that it is Ruth's homecoming celebration I want to remember. I ask Josey to stand. I take up the blanket, shake it free of sand, and fold it neatly, as I have done a hundred times. I place the blanket on the hot embers and a restraining hand on Josey's arm.

When the blanket has burned to a dulled memory, Josey smothers the fire. We gather the remainder of our day and walk back to where we left the truck. I hand her the keys, and she drives us back along the nearly deserted highway.

I balance two perfectly matched conch shells across my knees, and although I may have spared Ruth pain, even the possibility of a violent death, I was wrong to have insisted on her silence. She knew we weren't fooling anybody who really mattered. I now believe the moment in the cemetery when I traced our names on the tombstone, she touched me in forgiveness.

Josey leans and kisses me on the cheek.

"Figure I must taste like a salt lick."

"No, ma'am. You taste good, like warm butter."

Feels good. I miss kisses.

OH DEATH

Minnie Bruce Pratt

He sang, *Oh death! Oh death! Won't you*
pass me over for another day? She said, *I*

dreamed of you last night. I dreamed you
were telling me your whole life story.

Whole. Whorled. Welkin, winkle, wrinkle.
The loop of time holds us all together.

The pile of laundry on the bed. You
folding socks one inside the other. We
have had this day, and now this night.

The clothes are put away, and from the bed we see
the moon folding light into darkness, not death.

BLUE MOON

Minnie Bruce Pratt

The trees creak overhead, squeaky doors pushed forth
and back in the wind. On the porch we watch the moon
rising from whisper to guess to peach, white, then blue.

Once in a blue moon a love like this comes along.

We weren't standing alone. Lots of people, a room vast
with politics and that ex-lover playing catch-my-eye.
You read us a story, the one who had been you. A past,
the one who had been me. Your torn shirt, my needle's eye.

We had been alone. We had read what the other had asked.
The light shone on the pages, your face up-tilted in the glare.
Glory, mirror, future. Later I knew you were looking up at me.

I knew you, you knew me. We looked at each other,
shining on each other. Shining-on sun. Sailing-on moon.

THE GREAT SWAMP

Minnie Bruce Pratt

That spring you and I leaned over the edge,
staring into the swamp. What was in there?
Amphibian eyes glinting like treasure in the water,
gold dots of pollen flecking a sodden carpet.

That spring we saw you were beginning to die.
The arrowhead leaves flew slowly up green
out of the murky water. You got sick and sicker.

We leaned. Our shadows reached into the water.
We looked down into the mud, to where we'd seen,
to where what could be, lived, waiting to come.

THE HALLWAY OF THE FUTURE

Minnie Bruce Pratt

I type *life expectancy* out onto the keyboard.

The end is never definite, so we drove to the lake
and walked into the impending storm. I don't want
to rush this part. We were very happy, the huge
warm breath of west wind damp on our faces.

And then we sat in the car and held hands
while the rain shook its silver tasseled grass.

But this morning, your gaunt sleeping face,
the line of your body disappearing into the bed.

When I step out the door to go to work, I'm in
the hallway of a future without you. When I go
to get morning coffee what I drink is grief,
and at the bottom of the paper cup is loneliness.

UP SO EARLY

Minnie Bruce Pratt

Light dawns quickly on the computer screen.
You play me a song before I go off to work.

The song sings: *Not there, not there anymore.*
The people we were, there, are gone forever.

What we are not now—Not urban dancers,
not the couple practicing our perverse moves
in the black-and-white diner aisle, not the us
scrambling like rain through police barricades
in Times Square, not the me clasping white roses
escaped through an iron fence in the Village.

Goodbye, goodbye, the ones I've loved.
So long, our last life fading, video ending.

Behind us the rising sun casts its red stare
upon our wall. The shadow of what is here.
Lamp, leaf, bird. But not us, not yet.
Even though we are ready, and up so early.

HAND, HANDLE, LATCH

Minnie Bruce Pratt

We come back to the window, again, again. The moon
climbs ivory, peach, chrome yellow, and buttons
up the darkening blue sky over the valley. We lie down
as a line of sweat sews a seam, my wrist to your back.

No sleep, no sleep. Fear opens a door, some moment you
are gone from beside me. Chris told me the story at work:

One morning she stepped out her door in the country,
and feathers fumbled all over her yard—bronze, brown,
black, red—and the small limp bodies plucked
by fox, raccoon, coyote-dogs. A child had left
the gate open. I see that gap, no more than a breath.

I reach out to pull the gate closed. Hand, handle, latch.
Lock against whatever hides and waits to come into our room.

THROUGH THE GRAVEYARD

Minnie Bruce Pratt

Now we are half-way through the long fall.
Some leaves, those flakes of fire, smolder
under our feet as we take our afternoon walk.

Through the graveyard we talk about panorama,
perspective. In the labyrinth of turns we prefer
at each we have a choice, and at our back
a blue-black smoke of cloud is beautiful, whether
or not we are overtaken, going home to shelter.

HOURGLASS

Minnie Bruce Pratt

All night the wind throws sleet against the glass
like the sand stinging our faces and hands the day
the hurricane's tail end lashed us at the beach.

Time tumbles us back and forth in its giant hourglass.

One night at the beginning you stood naked in the hall,
it was storming outside the window, lightning, hail.
You flicker into light, arriving before me, once, again.

Time rattles at our window, time trying to get in.

BLISS

María DeGuzmán

May I some day, at the exit of grim understanding,
sing out jubilation and praise to affirmative angels!

— Rainer Maria Rilke, "The Tenth Elegy"

After a bad break up accompanied by more than one kind of betrayal, I had been in search of bliss, something to do more than take the pain away. You never know where bliss lies. It is much harder to find than opiates such as alcohol, drugs, non-stop dancing to the frenetic beat, sex, hedonistic partying, or sleeping too much. *Of this I cannot speak for fear of exposing it to mockery and contempt.* I learned that the hard way, but it would seem that I still have not learned the lesson. Or perhaps I know only too well and yet am willing to take the risk … If only to convince myself by confession that something about an encounter with a personality of rare complexity was sacred and worth salvaging even while that encounter left me surer than ever of the tragic nature of human affairs. How does one repair damage? Or does it merely accumulate, a growing pile of rubble from which emanates a mighty wind? Blowing the angel of history backwards while another angel steps lower and closer, takes us suddenly to her heart, to slay us with a kiss?

Here I am, trying to tell … to share an experience so that it will survive my own potential forgetting and my own certain mortality. Sharing the unshare-able while the feeling of remembering her— the grain of her drawl, the deliberateness of her stories, the slow amble of her gait, the way in which she closed personal space the better to hear me—is still alive in the deepest grooves of my mind. The cynical old world will insist that all memories—even the most powerful—become muted and fade over time. Had I not seen memory loss already from first-hand experience in the memory wards of assisted living facilities and nursing homes? And, yet, I had also witnessed surprising lucidity about the past. Memory thrives on distance imposed by the consequences of actions dragging away, on an iron chain, what should have remained within reach of a warm hand and parted lips.

It was at such moments of lucidity about the past that I would feel a wry smile break across my face like the smile she often directed at me, her head inclined toward mine and her eyes penetrating mine from under her arched brows. She would flash this smile at me as she told me one of her numerous tales of being a traveling saleswoman on the road around the Southeast. The tales were more than a tad risqué but tinged with irony and sadness at the world that early on had dealt her a mortal blow in the form of a fatal car crash that left her orphaned. The tales revolved around how to outwit sleazy, cheating men who would proposition her while simultaneously trying to get the better of her in a business deal. In each case, she would emerge the heroine--no let me amend that--the hero. She would rap her beautiful, large, bony, prominently veined hand upon the restaurant table at which we were seated to underscore exactly how she put that man in his place. And each time she put one of these men in his place I had the feeling that she was striking back at someone much closer to her in her past ... a brother who beat her, a neighbor who molested her. She told me that all her life she had had to fight. Trailing my gaze from her finely chiseled face with its broad forehead, deep-set eyes, and firm jaw to her broad shoulders, I had no reason to doubt her.

I was more than willing to hero worship her. Being an artist and an aesthete as much as a scholar and an activist, I had what I have come to consider a persistent longing for a muse descended from the code of chivalric romance with which I had been infected, most likely as a child, growing up around a Mediterranean world. A Mediterranean world filtered through the eyes of my expatriate American mother whose favorite writer was F. Scott Fitzgerald and his books populated by beautiful and merciless women who spurred the male protagonists on some quest for the romantic equivalent of the Holy Grail.

She had all the trappings of a muse. She was larger than life. She knew it, too. Once she remarked with a curious mixture of pride and self-directed faintly damning irony, "You may have noticed I do everything in a grandiose manner." She was tall, strong yet elegant. She had elegant bones. She was droll and dark and seemingly warm all at the same time. She could be stern, but when she smiled her eyes twinkled, indulgently. This is usually said of older people. And older she was. And this was part of the irresistible appeal, at least to me. That she seemed to be a repository of memory, exactly the sort of person who would not forget or at least wanted you to remember because something was, in fact, worth remembering. This, despite the fact that one evening she showed me around the guest bedrooms and other portions of her house as if she had never shown them to me on a previous evening. During the first house tour, she had led me past a set of photographs and clippings of herself framed along one wall. She appeared so different in each photograph that I had to stop and study them to assure myself that each of them was indeed of her.

The respect for memory that she bodied forth with her drawn out stories of decades of experience was set oddly ajar by her taste for massive furniture gilded in pale silvery gold and pastel tones imitating those found in eighteenth century French paintings. I forgave these affectations and allowed her to suspend me in her vertiginous mixture of nostalgia, melancholy, desire, and determination. The desire was hers for everything that had been beyond the reach of her family background and the circumstances in which she grew up. The desire was for life—more life!—in spite of and because of privation, ugly struggles, and, later, horror. And, the desire was mine for her desire, for her will to survive and her appreciation of literature, music, and beauty.

Yes, this is what I wanted—not just a friend and a lover, but, moreover, a muse. I have been one of those Nick Carraway types distractedly opening the door for the Jordan Bakers of the world as long as I get to gaze on Gatsby. An idolatrous and dangerous desire that persisted despite my years of dedication to detailed analysis of observable patterns and my commitment to the underdog and social activism. Dialing through radio stations one late evening of a half moon riding high in the sky I caught snatches of a radio preacher warning against the worship of idols. Let me ask you this: What happens when you meet a hard working underdog who burns to beat the system at its own game yet seeks to convince you at every turn that he or she is honorable and has a heart of gold? It was not the houses, cars, tasteful high-end clothes, and charities that lured me. It was not the lucre, though you may not believe me for a second. It was the thought that she needed nothing from me—as there was nothing I could offer her that she did not already have—except for my company, for my burning ears ever turned toward her mesmerizing mouth from whence proceeded that smile that made you feel as if you were the only one in the world. The only one in a world tilting madly on its axis, made all the bleaker by a recent break up accompanied by more than one kind of betrayal, and smelling of ashes and rotten flowers.

Into this personally catastrophic time stepped, at first diffidently and then what appeared to be boldly, this elegant, mysterious woman with her stories of survival against the odds and her love of literature, biographies, conversation, and whatever remained youthful in me despite my recent bitter disenchantments and my dread of the future. Her attraction to my youthful looks and what was left of my youthful heart would often manifest themselves like this: a friendly sock in the arm as she flashed me a radiant smile and looked at me sideways out of her shining eyes. I was in all senses of the word "disarmed." Was this her defense against the undertow of intense feeling that I, at least, could not stop myself from sensing was carrying us both toward somewhere neither of us had been before? When she would laugh and play the buddy role, I heard my own laughter rising girlishly in my throat. I felt younger than I had in years. I had the sneaking suspicion that she did, too. She kept calling me and spending time with me every week, even though early on she had put me off by informing me that she was ambivalently attracted to me as I was not, I gathered through her fragmentary comments, her usual eye-candy-on-your-arm type. But, though older than her usual targets, I did have the advantage of looking younger and healthier than they did. I had met some of them. And this youth and health she coveted.

I will not forget the late October afternoon I was leaning over a pool table trying to absorb my dark thoughts about the present and the future into the business of carefully aligning the cue to the ball to send it careening across the promising green baize. The cell phone rang in my pocket. It was she. She said, "I've been thinking about you, about what you told me. About feeling like an orphan who will be all alone when your parents die. That then you will be alone in the world." "Alone" sounded even lonelier in her slow drawl. She was referring to a remark I had made several weeks earlier. Her remembrance of it and her deliberateness in isolating it caught me off guard. As I stood still, heart pounding, with the pool cue in one hand and the phone up against my ear, she said in a low, serious voice, "You are not alone. Nor will you be alone. You have me. I'm here. And I will be here for you."

We had not known each other very long, and I scarcely knew how to take these statements. But, as every evening spent with her had been marked by a latent, if not sometimes overt, intensity despite the banter, I decided to take them at face value. Several weeks later, as I was driving home in the late afternoon, she called me and reiterated them again, as if she herself had determined that I not overlook them. I understood these statements to be part of a pledge of allegiance that placed her in the position of my emotional and creative benefactor. I hardly minded playing the vassal, the young, small-boned knight to this elegant queen. I would have gladly knelt before her except that both times she made these remarks we were on the phone.

One evening she invited me over to her place for dinner and a movie. I brought an attaché case of DVDs of American and European films. Without raising an eyebrow at my choice of container, she pulled out each DVD and read its back cover. She sat on the enormous couch in her living room, one long leg crossed over the other, turning each DVD case over in her prominently veined hands. She chose HBO's *Angels in America* and motioned me to sit down next to her. Not at one end of the couch. Right next to her. We could have been six feet apart at either end of this enormous couch, but wound up not even half an inch apart. Thigh to thigh we sank back into the middle of the couch that faced a wide wall-mounted high-definition flat screen. It was a cold mid November evening. She kept a throw on the couch that she spread over us so that we would stay warm during that long, two-part, film. She had settled in for the night. I wondered where this evening would end as I had a long drive home ahead of me. She seemed unconcerned about whatever was coming next.

She turned off her living room lights and there we sat while the film sent us sailing through the clouds over Golden Gate Bridge from west to east across the country toward Central Park and the colossal angel at the center of a fountain in the middle of the park. One or both of us shifted and then there was no physical space at all between us. The film had taken us to a synagogue and to a funeral and to the question of memory in the making of meaningful connections between people and to the relationship between two young gay men who were long-time partners but whose relationship was about to be sorely tested by the imminent revelation that one of the men has AIDS. One revelation flowed into another in the delirious dream that is the film version of Tony Kushner's two-part play. A disintegrating Mormon marriage between a closeted, Republican attorney, who winds up working for right-wing fixer Roy Cohn, and his valium-addicted wife. Cohn's ruthless attempts to cover up his own homosexuality and his illness from AIDS so as to retain his access to power and his ability to persecute his liberal, progressive, and radical opponents, and anyone he suspected of homosexuality. Cohn's seduction of the closeted gay Mormon attorney into the service of his own nefarious political designs. The abandonment of the young man with AIDS by his partner who then takes up with the attorney who then actively lies to his already nervous-wreck of a wife who suffers, sex-starved, from the sad sham of their marriage. Roy Cohn's physical illness and mental derangement from the AIDS virus that eventually causes him to hallucinate about visitations from the dead Ethel Rosenberg who he prosecuted as a Soviet spy and damned to the electric chair. The angelic visions of the young man abandoned by his partner who cannot cope with the realities of AIDS. The intensely erotic connection between this young gay man and the larger than life angel, played by Emma Thompson, who visits upon him tormenting ecstasies. The screen was aflame ...

Meanwhile, I sat beside my mysterious friend in my own crucible. I was acutely aware of her body pressed against mine. I did not dare to break the spell. And so we sat, breathing in the darkness, while the flat screen bloomed before us and the soundtrack washed over us. Sight and sound together poured these potent national and personal dramas into our heads, stirring each one of us toward some inevitable reflections on our own relation to them and, perhaps, to each other. This posture, held for hours to the point that she removed the throw, claiming she was hot—but not lessening the physical distance between us—left me light-headed. When at the film's end she murmured that she could not believe how late it was, that she had completely lost track of time, and that it was time for "this old girl to go to bed," I struggled to my feet, trying to conceal my whirling emotions, and announced, more for myself than for her, that I should return home and let her sleep. She grinned, accompanied me to the front door, held me in a longish embrace on the doorstep, and watched me silently as I got into my car and drove away. In my rear view mirror, I could see that she was still watching my car already halfway down the street. I knew she had gotten under my skin, into my blood. The angels seize nothing but what is theirs, or do they? A bit of one's own self floating in their tides of light, or was it darkness? That night I did not sleep a wink.

The following week she invited me over to her house again. For dinner and to spend time together. I tried to not anticipate what that might mean. She called me as I was driving to her house. She wanted to be sure I was arriving at the time we had agreed. I arrived early, got out of my car, and began to stroll around her secluded, upscale neighborhood. She drove past me and waved and within five minutes rang me on my cell phone. She seemed anxious that I return to her house. I briskly walked back to her place. She was standing in her driveway, waiting for me. When she saw me she gave me a wide smile and hugged me to her. Again, another lingering embrace. We stepped inside her house and she informed me that she wanted to take a shower and change her clothes for dinner and that I should wait for her in the living room. She switched on the large flat-screen play station on which we had watched the film telling me to please watch this television report for her and that she would be joining me shortly. The report was a commemoration of Kennedy's assassination in Dallas. It was then that I remembered what day it was: November 22.

She disappeared for a while, first downstairs where I could hear her talking on a phone to someone. Then upstairs where she was supposedly taking a shower and changing her clothes. The phone kept ringing periodically. The murmur of conversation was just out of earshot, especially with the television on, its volume turned up high. Higher than was necessary. Time passed. I left the living room area and stretched my legs in the kitchen and then drifted into a hallway and an alcove behind the kitchen. I returned to the living room and began perusing the books in her bookcases—histories, biographies, memoirs, novels. *Vivian Grey*. Next to it *Contarini Fleming*. Disraeli. And more than one biography of Disraeli.

Disraeli, buried in a vault beneath the Church of Saint Michael and All Angels, his last words having been, it was rumored, the *Shema*.

Just as my fingers grazed the key inserted into the lock of a book cabinet, I heard a footfall on the stairs. I turned around and she was already in the living room, staring in my direction. The stare broke into another smile. "I'm here," she said and motioned me to follow her.

We went out to dinner. She seemed less sure of herself that evening. She told me more stories about sleazy businessmen and about what she really wanted to do with her remaining time: run for political office or go on the campaign trail with a Democratic candidate, help others, learn to play the piano. I dropped my gaze from her face to her hands, palms down on the dark wood of the restaurant table, inches from mine. I murmured my encouragement and offered to give her some rudimentary lessons. She moved her hand over mine, held it there. I, very lightly, laid my free hand over hers holding mine. Time froze. Then she looked up, a slight flush in her otherwise pale cheeks, and a mischievous half-smile flickering on her lips, and said, "Ah, where were we?" We released each other, and she told me another story drawn from her past.

Back at her house, we again sat on the enormous sofa, this time with plenty of space between us. She was leaving the next day on a business trip further south and still had to pack. I got up to leave. Again she accompanied me to the front door.

I leaned toward her and kissed her right cheek. She reached out and crushed me to her, then held me away, and said, "I'm ambivalent, you know." This remark brought a hot flush into my face. I retorted, "Ambivalent about love?" I added, "I'll miss you." She looked at me and kept on looking, even after I was halfway down the street.

During the week she was out of town, she called me twice, both times after 10 PM at night. Two days before she returned home, she texted me way past midnight right before, she indicated in her note, she was going to sleep: "Getting sleepy. Wish you were here." I replied, "Wish I were there, too."

A week later she joined me for a dinner at a large anonymous restaurant along the highway, a surprise party for some mutual acquaintances. She arrived early to the party and stayed by my side the whole evening. It took no coaxing. She seemed wary of the other people and would occasionally whisper an amusing and slightly wicked comment in my ear about the proceedings. She hinted that I was the only one she respected, but I could not help feeling that I was leading a large lion around on a delicate, golden chain. I was also half-expecting that she would declare herself exhausted and leave. But, she did not. She seemed to be waiting for me to signal the next move. I suggested we go to a discotheque. To my surprise, she assented, strangely tame. At the disco she was not so tame and preferred throwing darts at a dart board to dancing. She refused to dance with me but she watched me dance with others for a while. Then, without warning, she was stalking for the door. I hastened off the dance floor, grabbed my coat, and followed her into the icy late November night. Once out in the street, she seemed docile and allowed me to take her arm and lead her to our cars. She wanted to go somewhere else, somewhere where we could talk.

We wound up at a wine bar and sat there for three hours drinking hot tea, conversing, and looking out onto the deserted streets of that postindustrial Southern downtown on that icy late

November night turning into December. We huddled over our teas, knees bumping under the table. She seemed preoccupied by something financial that she explained only in the most cryptic terms. As far as I could tell, it boiled down to cash flow problems with one of her businesses. Nothing particularly unusual, though I was trying to tally it up with her lifestyle. Nor was this the only aspect of her life with which she seemed dissatisfied. She admitted ruefully that she had been paternalistic in her love for other women, much younger than herself. Eye candy on her arm. She eyed me. I eyed her back. Suddenly she blurted out half-jokingly, "What would you and I do together, be boys together?" I seized my opportunity and said, "You need a love like that of David and Jonathan." I meant a love of equals, though one was older than the other. And, I admit, I meant much more. She did not blink. She did not turn away. She looked at me. I looked at her.

It was now 2 am. The bar was closing. We left, walking side by side. I offered her my arm to help her down some stairs, but she refused. We walked on together until we reached the parking lot where we had left our vehicles. The parking lot was deserted except for our two cars and one other. A freezing wind was whistling in our ears. I was shivering and my teeth were chattering. She unlocked her car, climbed into the driver's seat, and invited me to sit next to her. She turned on the heat and remained very still, her eyes watching an African American couple walking arm in arm across the lot to their car.

I was leaving the country for several weeks, and I felt a certain urgency to clarify things. I reached over and laid my left hand on the back of her right one. She turned her hand over, palm up. Our hands locked, palm to palm. I whispered hoarsely, "May I—." My words died away as she leaned toward me and brought her lips to mine. A long open-mouthed kiss. Time wound down to where it had been winding all along. I closed my eyes, riding some inconceivably powerful wave, suspended in a luminous darkness, a place I had always, always wanted to find—as if all my life were telescoping to this surprising point of joy. After a while, she drew back and said softly in her slow drawl, "That was nice." Now I was shaking, but not from the cold, rather from the impact of this encounter. All I could manage was to nod in agreement, bid her goodnight, press my burning palm against the frosty window of her car and lip-synch a reminder that she let me know when she was safely home. Through the glass, she smiled at me, that smile that made you feel as if you were the only one in the world. I got into my car. We drove our separate ways.

On my drive home, I kept replaying her words from many weeks earlier: *"You are not alone. Nor will you be alone. You have me. I'm here. And I will be here for you."* These words sealed by that kiss were now flooding me with the utterly euphoric restoration of a belief in intimacy as unity. That belief was surely the longed-for knowledge contained in the Garden of Eden's apple. Not the knowledge of good and evil that yielded, after one (or two) fateful bites, the realization of physical nakedness, emotional separation, and the experience of death. Instead, *this*, what I felt when her lips touched mine. The thrilling, self-annihilating mystery of unity with something divine in the other person. Yes, I realize now, looking back, *this is what was at stake*. This is why time burned with her as if it did not exist. This was her gift, her gift of bliss. This feeling of intimacy as unity with which I was graced one windy, ice-cold November night at the end of that fall, at the end of that year of betrayal, in which I met her.

During my time out of the country, we spoke every couple of days by phone at her request. During one of those calls, we arranged to meet for dinner when I got back. I tried not to build this meeting up, but, of course, that was next to impossible under the circumstances.

The night I arrived back in the country, she did not call. She texted she had had a long, rough day and that we would talk soon. I was disappointed not to hear the grain of her voice but continued to anticipate our meeting.

The night before we were supposed to meet she texted she was ill and that she would have to postpone until the following week. She promised to talk soon. The following week brought nothing but silence. No phone calls, no texts, nothing. I felt sick but there was nothing physically wrong with me. Meanwhile, the weather was alternately rainy and icy, one overcast day sliding into another, the southern roads treacherous with sleet, black ice, and fog.

The following week, in a text she reappeared: "Still recovering. Must stay out of this weather. Will call Christmas Day."

Christmas Day passed and no call. No word of any kind. Nothing the next day or the day after that. Everything inside of me was spiraling downwards in a steep descent of disbelief, denial, and sorrow. New Year's Eve and New Year's Day came and went. Still no word, no call. Nothing.

The weeks passed and I left messages for her that went unanswered. I learned from some mutual acquaintances that she was alive. But they had not been able to spend time with her either. From active pursuer and collector of the people who had interested her, she turned evasive.

It became known that she had closed one of her businesses. Then, it was rumored that she had declared bankruptcy and was selling another of her businesses. A few months later her house was on the market. Perhaps other properties of hers would be soon. She was selling and moving further south. Much further south.

I wondered about her five or ten or fifteen years into the future. I pictured her driving out to some lonely jetty along the Gulf of Mexico in one of her luxury vehicles. She would park her car and get out to stretch her long legs. Her deep-set eyes would be dimmer but still captivating, aligning themselves with the distant horizon line. Her face would still be that of a Blakean angel turned into the wind blowing off the Gulf. She would move, pensive and slow, all the time fixing her gaze on the waves rippling between herself and that distant horizon. Her face would be inscrutable.

And I? Would I still be pacing in cramped circles, over and over, softly pacing as if in a ritual dance around this quiet catastrophe, my will suspended before that illuminated darkness rushing wordlessly between my parted lips that icy November night and plunging into the shadowy depths of this heart of mine? And would I still be haunted by that half-forbidden, elusive moment of apparent grace and solidarity between us and by the double-edged, flaming gift she gave to me that I have not been able to forget?

STRIP HER

Danielle Bero

Passion fruit lotion
coats
her skin like a cell
membrane
smooth, lubed

her hair tentacles
suction
black pupils snack on the hazel
highlights

frosted
I can smell her taste
Hips separate from her body
rotates, pops, bounces
hydraulics on a Cadillac

tart violent carbonated sips
gulps

She glides up and down my jeans
leaving slug trails
shimmers
around my zipper

She cups my hands over
her bare breasts
and whispers over my neck
Trey Songz lyrics

cut in tacky lines
of white powder suck
I open her mouth with
my delicate fingers

Slide folded bills down her throat
use the remainder to wipe tear ducts

LETTER TO A MEMORY

Arya F. Jenkins

She was the one
The first
The golden one
Goldmund to my
Narcissus
And as we slept together
Seasons changed
I realized I was not myself
But part of her
Dreaming
Not knowing nearly well enough
Who she was
How she felt
Our tendency always being
To remake love in our image

She was hungrier than I was
And more beautiful
If there was beauty in me
It was fire and although it
Was invisible
I burned believe me I
Burned until I cracked open
And learned to weep real

She was there when I was
No more than a seed
An idea she
Pulling
Pushing
Tending

All I wanted was our time together
Alone silent
She over me
Her soft cheek and angled hair
Sweeping over me
Her breasts meeting mine
Nipple to nipple
I was the canvas on which she
Fathomed a future

I couldn't fathom
Anything but running
Fucking drinking
Abandoning the world I had known
That was trying to break me

I left for Provincetown
And she for academia
And pages turned us
Away from one another

Then one day
We met again
Me asking her forgiveness
For a cruel break up
I had never even wanted

She told me then
She was going through
A *great change*
But couldn't explain more
Years after that a mutual friend
Informed me she had changed gender

I remembered then
When we first met
She had said
Do you ever feel
You're someone else inside
Which I took to be
A come-on
Nothing more
Because to me it seemed obvious
She was gay
Like me

And so it comes to pass
The mirror breaks
The shards cut my own
Sex separating me from the
First one
The one I truly loved
Always
Taking her from my heart
And memory forever

She is gone
I mourn her again
And who he is now
Is not mine anymore
Even if in his eyes
I still see the warm
And smiling traces
The ruins of what
He once loved.

ROCKING

Carla Tomaso

Deb was sitting on her front porch thinking about what else she could have done with her life. She'd done a lot; it wasn't that. She'd been married three times. She'd taught world literature, played competitive tennis, written poetry, loved dogs. Between husbands she'd travelled throughout Europe, Asia and South America.

She wasn't exactly dissatisfied. She just didn't feel quite herself yet.

But who ever does, really? Except Buddhist monks and Olympic athletes maybe.

The problem is that you get to be seventy and everybody thinks you're done, that you ought to sit in a rocking chair and smile at the people who walk by.

Today Deb was contemplating opening a restaurant called *The Wasteland* where everything was philosophical.

She took out her tiny notebook and wrote down some menu items.

The Existentialist, for example, was whatever the chef found in the refrigerator that couldn't wait.

The Kafka wasn't a cockroach but a lightly battered grasshopper, crispy with a little paprika sauce on the side.

Then there was *Love*, something indescribable, savory and sweet, a borscht perhaps with rose blossoms drifting on the surface.

The phone rang. It was Janis, her oldest child, the one who had taken it upon herself to watch out for Deb.

"Hi Mom," Janis said, chewing something, probably a piece of toast. This was her morning check-in call, a major bore. But if Deb didn't answer now she'd just have to talk later or worse. Janis might insist on stopping by.

"Hi honey," Deb said into her cell. "What's up?

"I'm at the market. Need anything?" Janis shouted at her, like they were both deaf.

"I need love," Deb said. "Can you pick me up some of that?"

"Is that a dishwashing soap?"

Janis wasn't exactly brilliant, nor did she have much of a sense of humor. So why did Deb tease her, poor thing? She felt bad about it, but she kept on doing it anyway.

There was a silence.

"You're teasing me, right?" Janis said.

"Yes and no," she said. "I'm sorry. I don't want anything. You don't need to stop by."

"Deborah's got a tap dance recital this afternoon if you want to come."

This was the oldest granddaughter, dutifully named after her.

"Not this time," Deb said. Tap dancing adults always made her laugh and there was no telling what a bunch of percussive children would make her do.

"Well, call me if you get lonely."

"I will, dear."

Her children had insisted she leave Boston to live near them in her fading years. She knew it was probably a good idea but it still peeved her. Why was aging such a pain in the ass? It should be the best of times, not the worst, not Dickensian but full of tender moments and hearty laughter. She'd hoped the move west would provide her with some new experiences and at least a few intelligent people she could talk to.

So she'd bought this yellow house with a big porch where she could sit and write in her notebook and wait for something to happen.

She didn't miss anybody really although one of her favorite experiences had been a visit to London focusing on the Bloomsbury group with a bunch of teachers from New England. They were all in love with Virginia, Vanessa, Clive, Lytton etc. etc. Deb admired

Virginia Woolf too but didn't envy the depths of her depression and mania culminating in that sad drowning. But who could resist the idea of Thursday night salons, the devotion to art and writing, the complicated love affairs, the comfortable houses and Vanessa's dreamy paintings decorating the fireplace of her house, Charleston?

Since her sloppy fall in Boston last spring, Deb had given up drinking and taken up pot supplied to her by an ex-student with whom she'd kept in touch. He mailed baggies and papers to her in a hollowed out hardcover copy of *Moby Dick* that she emptied and returned dutifully with fifty bucks enclosed. Back and forth across the United States flew Melville's novel, one of Deb's least favorite.

"Call me Ishmael," intoned the seafaring narrator on page one, as he began to describe crazy Captain Ahab's man-journey to conquer the angry whale.

Men were such children. Children who couldn't bear children and had to conquer things like whales and mountains and innocent women.

She wasn't rabid but she was a feminist. Her sons teased her about it in a gentle way to show her how it amused them, their old mother having a political agenda that seemed to exclude them.

Deb found a joint in her pocket and lit up. It was still only mid-morning but she wanted a couple of hits. Her mind worked better on pot. Her thoughts interested her. They flew higher and went deeper both at the same time.

She thought about Emma, the only grandchild she felt close to at all. She'd paid for a big family trip to Maui last Christmas and ended up wishing she'd just taken Emma, the only one who seemed to give a damn about her. She was ten, the youngest and smartest and most sensitive of all of them. Emma held Deb's hand during the entire double zip line excursion that came with the vacation package. Not for herself but for Deb, who had suddenly developed a fear of heights and everything else the zip line included.

"I've got you, grandma. It's OK, I won't let you go."

The memory made Deb want to cry.

Soon Emma would grow up and emulate her silly older sisters with their makeup and tiny skirts and obsession with boys. She'd start to shave every hair on her body except maybe her head. She'd flip her curls, gaze at her image in mirrors and windows, always outside herself, always feeling the awful pressure to re-create her body and mind to please the rest of the world.

Goodbye Emma.

That was how life worked. You had something good and it was gone the same moment. Good, gone.

Her first husband James had died of cancer. He was the gentlest, most loving man she'd ever met and pop, a year after they married he showed her this lump on his back. The rest of the brief marriage was about his dying and her grief.

The thing that killed her about losing him was that, even in all his pain and fear, he knew how to listen and how to ask her the questions that mattered.

The children came with her marriage to Ed, a harmless, pointless guy who was as safe as shit. Janis was his spitting image.

He was healthy and kind to her but he couldn't carry on a conversation to save his life. Still, he didn't expect a thing back which gave her the opportunity to sleep around experimentally and neglect her kids a little bit. She still felt guilty about that but not too much. Deb left him after the kids grew up which made everybody hate her for a while.

The third husband, a bad boy who was good in bed, paid her back double time with girlfriends and shitty luck. She barely got out of that one alive.

She'd never told anybody about the worst of it. She just didn't see herself as a battered, bullied woman. When Craig broke her cheekbone, she left and moved in with Dot, her best friend, for a month or two, until the apartment next door opened up.

And that was the end of that.

Deb took her last puff, a deep one, blowing smoke out the side of her mouth so nobody on the sidewalk would smell it. A huge crow came swooping down and landed on top of the fence between her house and the house next door. The divorced mom and her teenaged daughter, who had both gotten pregnant at the same time of all things, had sold it and moved out.

She hadn't known them to speak to. Although the mother gardened sometimes early in the morning, their lives seemed to be all about men and sex. Deb could hear it sometimes when she was trying to get to sleep.

If she'd had the confidence to write a story or a sitcom those neighbors would have been a terrific premise. She would have treated their pregnancies gently though because sometimes, when young moms came back to visit her classroom with their toddlers in tow, they had had success stories to tell her about getting jobs and degrees. High school pregnancy could be extremely motivational.

"Caw," the crow said.

"This moment, stay this moment. You are all we have... (or something) ...never come again." She loved that quote from Virginia Woolf. She couldn't remember it exactly but it was on a calendar she'd pinned up next to her desk inside.

She would really have rather been a writer than anything else but what did she have to say?

Even that was a cliché.

She looked up. A child about Emma's age and a man were coming up her walkway, uninvited. They'd just pushed open the little gate as if they knew her. Were they Jehovah's Witnesses? Were they selling something else she didn't want?

"Hi," the man said. He was dressed like a golfer, casual but pressed. "How are you?" He reached out his surprisingly soft white paw for a shake.

Deb had to put out her joint in the ashtray first. He didn't seem to notice.

"I'm good," she said finally taking his had in hers. "I'm writing a novel."

"I'm Tom," he said. "And this is Scout."

Scout smiled engagingly. Deb couldn't tell if Scout was a boy or a girl.

"Do you have a dog?" the child asked.

"I'm sorry to say I don't. I did," Deb said. "Do you?"

"A dog is in the picture very soon," Tom said, rubbing his kid's hair. "This afternoon maybe. Now that we have a yard."

"Next door," Scout said.

"Where the crow is?"

Everybody looked at the top of the fence where Deb was pointing.

"Yes," Scout said.

The crow flew away, swooping and swerving as if it owned the sky.

"Oh," Deb said. "Good. I thought you might be selling something."

"Like religion?" Tom said, laughing.

Deb took a deep breath. This guy was funny. How amazing.

"You're funny," she said. "Wonderful."

"Don't you want to know about my name?" Scout said, sitting down on the steps to launch into it.

"*To Kill a Mockingbird*? Child of Atticus."

Scout shook Deb's foot lightly and beamed.

"Yes!!! How did you know?"

"I used to be an English teacher," she said winking at Tom.

"You've got to meet my mother," Tom said. "She's staying with us for awhile."

"Why should I meet her?" Deb said in spite of herself. "Because we're both old?"

"She's funny too," said Scout who was definitely a girl.

"I think you'd enjoy each other," Tom said pulling Scout up and starting back down the path to the street.

"I have a granddaughter named Emma," she called out to them. "She's about your age, Scout. She's my favorite. Maybe you two could hang out together sometime."

Scout turned around and glared at Deb.

"Why?" she said. "Because we're both young?"

"Oh, touché," Deb said.

"She'd love to play with Emma," Tom said, grabbing Scout's hand again.

Scout kicked a rock off the path.

"I don't get along with most girls my age is all," she said. She looked up and Deb noticed what beautiful blue eyes she had. Was she crying?

She and Emma would be perfect.

Deb went into her house, taking the ashtray and the tiny notebook.

She looked around. She'd lived here five or six months but sometimes the place seemed brand new. Wood floors, white walls, lots of bookcases and daylight. Craftsman-like, the realtor had called it. He'd been embarrassed by the old yellow tile in the bathroom and the white appliances in the kitchen.

"You can change them out," he'd said, waving his arms to encompass the whole house.

"Why would I do that?" Deb had said.

She'd liked the realtor, Brian. He was tall like her first husband had been. James, the one who'd died of cancer.

"You like old," he'd said happily. "Good for you. Most people seem to be frightened by it. They want stainless steel everywhere. Like a surgical unit."

"Or the morgue," Deb said.

She had a few paintings on the walls but not many photographs. She didn't need them. Her family she could see in person any time she wanted and photos of her dead relatives and friends depressed her.

Except for the one of her with James. She picked up the black and white photo from her desk. He had a long face, short, curly brown hair, tortoise shell glasses and a small smile. James with his long arm around her shoulders, Deb beaming hugely.

"I was so in love," she thought.

His head was a foot higher than hers, but his body was always ready to bend over her, like a stork.

She lay down on the couch and tried to fall asleep. She wanted to dream about James.

Later on the doorbell rang. The light outside was lower so Deb knew she'd slept. It must have been at least four o'clock. She got up slowly and opened the door.

It was Scout with an adorable dog on a leash. A little brown terrier mix who was jumping straight up and down with joy.

"And who have we here?" Deb said.

"Jasper," Scout said. "My dad and grandma and I just picked him up at the shelter. Come outside and see what he can do."

She went out to the porch and sat down on the top step. Scout unleashed the dog who began tenderly to lick a scratch on Deb's arm. She shivered from the warm touch.

"They like the salt in the blood," she said.

"Jasper. Fetch." Scout threw the yellow ball she had in her pocket. Jasper caught it on the bounce.

Deb clapped.

"Great dog," she said.

"I wanted to make sure you liked him," Scout said.

"Of course I like him. Who wouldn't?"

"Dad says it's important to have happy neighbors."

"Does your grandmother like Jasper?"

"Of course. She saw him first."

"Why did she move in with you?"

"I don't know," Scout said. "To cook maybe."

Jasper peed on a gardenia bush and then patted the ball back to Scout. What a dog. He almost made Deb want to get another one.

Scout threw the ball again and Jasper brought it back to Deb this time. Deb tossed it hard and by mistake it bounced into Scout's yard.

"Wow," Scout said. "You've got some arm."

"I used to play tennis," Deb said. "Bad aim though. It must have gone through the fence somehow."

Scout stood on the porch table and peered over it. Deb held on to her hand to steady her.

"Grandma," she called. "Could you get the ball?"

"So she moved in to cook?"

"She makes everything delicious," Scout said, jumping off the table. "Even fish. Her friend died so dad said she should stay with us for a while. My mother's gone somewhere else."

Deb glanced up and saw the grandmother looking back at her, her head just visible over the top of the fence. It was kind of eerie.

"Hey there," the grandmother said.

Deb studied what she could see of the woman's face. What wonderful intense blue eyes she had. Eyes like Scout. And that straight gray hair pinned back with silver barrettes. And the way she smiled. So welcoming. So true.

"I feel like I know you," Deb said, getting up to greet her.

It flew out of her mouth she felt the recognition so strongly.

"I'm Sally," the neighbor said.

It must have been the Virginia Woolf thing. Or James. The long slender face, the deep eyes.

"Are you standing on a box or something?"

"She's just tall," Scout said.

Deb walked to the fence and raised her arm as high as she could to shake hands. Sally caught hers and pressed. Her hand was big and warm like Tom's.

"Scout's been talking about you all day, "Sally said.

"I hear you make great fish."

"I have an idea," she said. "Step back."

She disappeared for a moment and then Deb heard a loud creak and slapping sound as two of the fence panels fell in toward her garden.

"What?" she shouted. "You kicked it in?"

Jasper started barking crazily and Scout ran to check things out. Deb couldn't move. She felt like she was cemented in place. She couldn't make any of her muscles work.

Scout returned laughing and holding Sally's hand like a courtier with her queen.

"She broke the fence so she could walk through."

Sally was a beautiful woman. And she was indeed tall and slender, wearing some kind of flowing green and purple top with a long black skirt. Of course. Just the way Deb had pictured her. A Bloomsbury gal.

"That was a great idea," Deb said.

"The fence was rotten right there," Sally said. "An impulse came over me. I hope you don't mind. I'll get it replaced. No vegetation was destroyed."

"No," Scout said, running across the fallen boards to her house. "This is so magic. We'll make it a secret opening, like in a story book."

Jasper chased her, his barking muted by the yellow ball in his mouth.

And then they were gone.

But Sally stayed, standing and waiting for Deb.

"Want a cup of tea?" Deb asked. "Or whatever."

She felt strangely shy and awkward.

"Do you have time for a visit?" Sally asked.

"That's what I've got," she said. "Time. Or wine or pot?"

"Everything," she said. "Surprise me. I haven't had a good surprise in ages."

"The fence falling in was a surprise to me," Deb said.

Sally laughed.

"Not in a bad way," Deb added.

She went inside while Sally rocked on the porch. She opened a bottle of wine, and grabbed the joint. Then she boiled water and made a pot of tea. What else? A few cookies, some sliced cheese and crackers. She carried everything out on her prettiest enamel tray. Although she'd promised herself to act casual and smooth, she was shaking just a bit.

"Take a deep breath or you'll scare her away," she said to herself.

She put the tray on the table and sat down in the other rocking chair.

"I'll start with tea," Sally said, her long legs crossed at the ankle in front of her.

She was so relaxed.

They each took a cracker and some cheese. They sipped their tea.

"Are you ever lonely?" Sally said at last.

"I've always been lonely, I think. Except for the first husband, James, who got sick and died almost immediately."

She began to tear up and wiped her eyes as fast as she could. She didn't want Sally to be put off by this stupid self-pity either.

Sally leaned toward her.

"I've been very lucky," she said. "My partner, Julia, and I were together for almost forty years. Not perfect of course but we were always friends. We enjoyed trusting each other."

Deb took a shaky sip of tea and spilled a little on her blouse, an ugly red and white striped thing she'd had forever.

"We raised Tom together," she added

Sally was telling her that Julia had been her lover. She was a lesbian.

"Tom is a nice man," Deb said.

"Julia, Tom and I lived on a ranch in Montana," Sally said.

"Cattle?"

"Sheep. Julia was a weaver. I was a doctor at a clinic in town. Most of my patients were Native Americans. When Julia died six months ago, Tommy asked me to come here for a while. He said he worried I would be lonely but I think it's more for him and Scout."

"The mother is gone for good?"

"Who knows? Neither of them wants to talk about her."

Deb thought about this. Why would anybody leave Tom and Scout? And how could Sally stop herself from asking them about it?

"Are you lonely?" she said. She passed Sally the Girl Scout Samoas she'd bought a few weeks ago from one of her granddaughters.

Sally gazed toward the front walk for a long time, evidently thinking about her answer. Even her profile was lovely, strong chin, aquiline nose. The barrettes were simple, silver Scandinavian oblongs with a bird etched in the center. A gift from Julia no doubt.

"I don't know. I sold the ranch. I miss the sheep."

Deb laughed.

"That isn't what I thought you'd say."

"Julia is with me still," Sally said, taking a bite of the cookie. "I haven't let her go yet. I talk to her every day."

Deb thought of James. She wondered what it would have been like if she'd had him for years and years. She'd never talked to him after he was dead.

"I lost my first husband so quickly," she said. "I can't imagine how you must feel."

"I think it might be easier if you've been able to have somebody a long time. You can be grateful." She took a sip of tea. "I don't want to cry right now."

So Deb told Sally about the other husbands, trying to make the worst of the stories quirky at least, sometimes funny.

It was getting dark out.

"Shall we go inside?" she said.

"Let's light some candles," Sally said as they went in.

Deb found a few and set them around the room.

"Now could we smoke some of your joint?" she said. "My patients gave me some once in a while, when they couldn't pay, but I haven't had any in years."

They inhaled, exhaled, coughed a bit and then did it all again.

Once, passing it back and forth, their fingers touched.

"Have you ever read Virginia Woolf?" Deb said after she stubbed out the joint.

Sally had. Her favorite was *To the Lighthouse*, the one where the house narrates the time going by. The one where Lily Briscoe, a young artist, falls in secret love with Mrs. Ramsay.

"It's mine too," Deb said with so much force her breath blew out one of the candles on the table between them.

Neither of them said anything after that. Deb relit the candle and felt content to watch it glimmer on the planes of Sally's face and on her silver barrettes. The small birds seemed to flutter in the light.

"I should go, I guess," Sally said finally.

"OK," Deb said, trying to sound neutral.

"Come over tomorrow to our place," Sally said.

"When?"

"Anytime. All day."

Deb's heart rolled over in her chest. This gal was so open. Who would ever say that, 'all day'?

"I think Scout would like my granddaughter Emma," she said.

Deb grabbed the flashlight she kept near the front door and they walked outside to the break in the fence. It looked different. Like a beautiful floral bower.

"That Scout," Sally said, clapping her hands. Deb ran the flashlight all over the opening. Scout had decorated it with luxuriant green vines.

"These look like passion fruit," Deb said, touching the foliage. "The former owner was a great gardener."

"Lucky for us," Sally said.

"Yes," Deb said. "It is."

Sally bent to kiss her lightly on the cheek. Deb shivered slightly as if she'd been asleep for years.

"I'll see you tomorrow," Sally said. "Bring your girl."

After dinner and a bath, Deb went to her desk and took down the Virginia Woolf calendar she'd pinned to the wall. She read the quote underneath the black and white photo of Virginia sitting in a lawn chair, drinking tea just months before killing herself.

"The great revelation perhaps never did come. Instead there were little miracles, illuminations, matches struck unexpectedly in the dark; here was one."

Deb got a pen and wrote "Sally", filling in the entire white square of the seventh of April, the next day. Then, after the name, in the space that was left, she put one exclamation point after another and another.

This was what she would do with the rest of her life. She would fall in love with a woman, this Sally, and it would finally be enough.

LOVING SAINTS

Petra Kuppers

I

Sophia, the mother of wisdom, the patron saint of alchemists. Jehovah's grandmother.

Orphea: Monique Wittig's singer who pulls her dead lover successfully from the
Underworld.

Madonna: pop icon, elusive object of desire in Desperately Seeking Susan. Also Virgin with large mantle for all mankind to shelter in.

Hermes: messenger of the gods, with winged feet, sly, swift, personifies alchemical knowledge. Roman name: Mercurius, gives his name to the philosophical mercury, quicksilver, the substance that puts alchemical processes into gear.

Beatrice Portinari: Florentine gentlewoman, Dante's muse, his guide through paradise in the Divine Comedy.

Mother Ann Lee: founder of the religious orders of the Shakers. Disapproved of sex, thought the Shakers should multiply through conversion. Shaking as prayer.

Olivia Newton John: a muse on skates, trying to enter Los Angeles and the (love) lives of mortals, ends up being a waitress.

II

I need to hear your voice, sweet one
I need to feel your footsteps
your wheels' path
your snaking ways
traverse over my own breast.
Show me the way

I will dry my arm pit hair in the public toilet
I will lie in the dirty tent at the street's side
I will skate to the muses with you.
Your voice is sweeter to me than the song of Saint Peter
that growling swell over an opulent grave
Gregorian chanting sets my neck hair on edge
your voice is sweeter than Beatrice
up there in the gods
in the outer theatre
on the big screen
open your coat to me
Sophia, guide me to her
guide me to the one who will reclaim her skin
                    and her soul in the fire.
Sophia, let me lie with you, at night
your skin is dark like the gorilla's,
and you sit patient on the sloping mountain-side
your skin is light like the face of a young Rhesus monkey,
and you scream with delight in the tops of the trees
your skin has the spots of a fawn,
and the bruises of too much bloodletting
be my mistress, Sophia, silent or screaming,
let me swim in your lymph,
let me climb onto your perfect red blood cells,
cuddle down in the hollowed out sphere
let me rest while I witness
your transhuman membranes
there she is, she who fights outwards, towards the light
she, the hero, will sing
oh my ears
oh your flow
oh Sophia,
let us see who will hear and who will answer.

III

Now you have pierced the storm cloud
    shred the membrane
    slash the lions and tigers
    circle, knife in hand,
    lightly on your feet
    full of the lightness
    honed to the blade
    dance and duck, duck weave
    you remember rock'n'roll
    in the rap gap of the knife edge
    rap trap
    weave in and out of the light
    flash on your hair
    then storm
    forward
    blood
    blood
        for a long time

        for a very long time there's the spray and the glow

        for a long time (brother) you stare at the sand

and the light leaks out and the rhythm
these feet loose their wings
gravity as the goddess flees from the scene
from your feet to your knees
the vortex of the sun coils its last dragon breath
your forehead moist on the gritty earth.

IV

In the juicy warmth of your disintegration, my beloved
Beloved, I try to hold on to
form
remember these borders

lands of the pasture
my garden Eden
form a new terra, here
initiate
take your magic,
and I wait, wait, deep inside my eternal friend.
Sophia shall rock me.
Here is my burden
flowing toxic in this blood.
I bless you, young one.
I bless you and give you nourishment for your path
no pure rinds
no manna
but the sweet flesh of my breasts.

V

They go up and down and up and down and we turn
wheels turn
spherical revolution
long cycle
cycle
cycle
cyclical revolution evolution radical radix the still
                              point of the turning
reach out to touch the skin as it passes by
the sound of the other
smell of skin
sun burns down on my nape
nape wings fly to you
flare to you like a bull protector
crown me
yoke me
parallel furrows

SELF-LOVE

Gabrielle Montesanti

The night I came out as a lesbian to my childhood friend, she responded by outlining her promise with God to remain abstinent until marriage.

"Ultimately it's your life," she said to me, "but I choose to remain pure."

In retrospect, I have no idea why chastity and my sexual orientation were tangled up in her mind, but I suspect it had something to do with the little Bible College she was attending at the time. It was nestled in a rural part of Michigan that I avoided by a span of fifty miles. By the time we turned 21 I'd encountered enough doomsday sermons and hellfire in my upbringing to justify my refusal to visit. She told me the college forced everyone to sign a chastity contract upon enrollment, and implemented strict rules that trapped men and women in separate dormitories after sundown.

"Once, this girl I know got in trouble when a boy sat on her bed to do homework," she told me.

"Well, how do they prevent gay sex?" I asked.

"Oh, homosexuals aren't allowed on my campus. Or at least they aren't allowed to talk about it," she said. "I mean, it's safer for everyone that way. There's also a strict filter on all internet connections for pornography and questionable websites like Victoria's Secret, so we can't be tempted."

It never occurred to me to use the Victoria's Secret website to masturbate. I imagined stripping down to my dirty pink bra and loose cotton underwear, fashioning a giant pair of angel's wings to my naked back and running out to the quad to gyrate on the statue of Mary Magdalene. I would ride it with a bottle of peach schnapps in one hand and the Holy Bible in the other. That institution would drive me to insanity, I was sure of it. "What's wrong with a little self-love?" I'd scream.

I came out of the closet that day like a race horse at the Kentucky Derby. I used sex the way she used Jesus. Instead of simply uttering the two words and moving on, I detailed my first sexual encounter like a paperback romance and watched her grow visibly uncomfortable. Her face contorted the way mine did when she prayed publically at restaurants and engaged our Biology teacher in a conversation about creationism. I could almost see her itching to hit the ground to pray on my behalf; I had grown familiar with that look of pity and shame.

My mother got me a Rastafarian hat for Christmas after I came out as a lesbian. It was green and black, like the hat Bob Marley slapped over his long dreads right before lighting a joint.

"You're kind of a hippie now, right?" she said. "This hat fits your new aesthetic."

By aesthetic, I figured she meant my sexual orientation, though to me there was nothing new about it. I am sure it felt like an abrupt change to her-- a semi-professional dye from chestnut brown to flamingo pink. It probably felt like a betrayal, an unspoken promise to follow a devout Catholic lifestyle I'd snapped in half with my knee.

"It's secretive," she told me once. "The lesbian lifestyle is so secretive, and I just want so much better for you."

I wanted to prove her wrong but for years I did the opposite. I constantly lied about where I was going and who was coming with me. When I came home from college for breaks, I waited for her to retreat to bed and then I creeped down to the basement, speckled with hardened cat vomit and littered with deflated yoga balls to talk to my girlfriend on the phone. I snuck out of the house to kiss her in the backseat of my '99 Taurus, parked outside the football stadium at my old high school. Then I snuck her back into my house and we had sex in my tiny twin bed with the snowman sheets.

Nothing seemed less appealing than the vow of chastity my friend described the day I came out. For years, she claimed it was easy to keep this promise to God, seeing as she possessed neither a love interest nor the urge to masturbate. A few months after my coming out, she approached me to tell me she would come to my gay wedding and gay reception, should I ever choose to get gay married.

"When I am a pastor I will risk my job for you," she told me. "Even though I don't respect some of the choices you have made, I will do it because I treasure our friendship so much."

A few months later, a Christian boy with a ponytail and a tie-dye bandana moseyed on into her Bible Studies class. When they started dating, she described how difficult it was to remain abstinent. Sleeping next to him on the couch, she learned to allow the lust to wash over her without allowing it any power. They kissed, I confirmed, and occasionally he slid his hands under her sweater, but they promised God that until marriage they would go no further.

Eventually, he convinced her it wasn't sex unless he came, which he did, one night in November.

"I hardly remember it," she told me gravely. "We were both fast asleep, and all of a sudden we were fully awake. It felt good to finally be touched, just for a moment, and then it was over. So, I just want to apologize for judging you all these years. It is very difficult to stay pure. Now I sin like you."

I laughed in her face and slapped on my Rastafarian hat.

"Nobody sins like me."

IN TONGUES (FOR SS, MAY 2015)

Cassandra Langer

Dare you speak
The pulse of your pussy
How it purrs
When you make love
To yourself

When you give
Your orgasm
To me

Dare I say
How good
The fullness
Of your breasts feel
In my hands

The full weight
Nipples rising
To meet my mouth
Makes my cunt moist
With longing for you along

Our perfect bodies fitting together
Halves streaming steaming
My hand on your belly
Yours pulling me into you
Rising falling
Love together
Here now always

COMPROMISE (MARCH 14, 2015 FOR SS)

Cassandra Langer

There is no absolute freedom
every question has an edge

Because you are lovely
here on the other side
of this equation
this eternity
you can tear through my heart
like a mistral all heated energy

You can ask me not to be angry
hold me in chains of imaginary kisses
recalling every real one we have shared
in our place outside of time

The transition a kind of
thickening distance
that must be bridged
as I remember you
between my thighs
the dappled light on your breasts
nipples rising to meet my mouth

My heart is not a turnstile
spinning in the cold light
of inevitable loss

I wake up in bed
to the cat's insistent
head butting my hand
dreaming the intervening space

The one that you and I cross
time and again when
your lips meet mine

How we manage
the sacrifices demanded
by the routine of impossibles
our reality demands

THE GIFT OF INVENTION

Hilary Holladay

It was possible because we were so thin and no one gave us a thought. We weighed about as much as a couple of paper dolls and had roughly the same value. Nobody, neither guard nor fellow prisoner, cared about us, two teenaged girls who didn't have a chance of surviving the winter. Barely more than shadows with white trails of breath coming out of our mouths and nostrils, we were starving like everybody else. J. had nearly died of typhus. But that winter, after my parents died and after J.'s parents were killed, she regained some strength and we began making plans to escape.

J. and I met practically as soon as I stumbled off the train from Kraków. I was a seventeen-year-old ethnic Pole, a professor's daughter who loved to draw and paint. She was a year younger and originally from Germany, the only child of two teachers who had immigrated to Warsaw. When her school was forcibly closed and her parents lost their jobs, she stayed home sewing and knitting and reading. Her father was reduced to scavenging for food on the streets at night. The family had been rounded up and deported just a day before that fate befell my parents and me.

Her eyes, a pale blue, hung on mine as if she had already decided we should stick together. She arrived just after they stopped shaving everybody's head—there were just too many people to keep doing that—but of course they would not let her keep the beautiful plait of thick golden-brown hair that trailed down her back. Her hair was soon cut short just like mine. But in my mind, I always saw it long, a braid she flipped from side to side.

And so we became friends. She held me the night my father died and again after my mother died, barely a week later. I held her when her parents were taken to the Wall and shot to death. That night, as her tears ran down my face to my collarbone, she pulled away for a moment and looked at me. *"Wir finden das Weg,"* she said. *We will find the way.*

A few weeks later, in the hellish cold of mid December, after the others around us fell into their rough, wheezing slumbers, J. and I began whispering our ideas back and forth. Given the chance to sleep, it was the rare person who did not. But we took extra precautions if by chance a traitor was only feigning sleep. We knew of no one else on our bunk or the two bunks below ours who spoke both Polish and German, so I spoke in Polish and she in German. That way, no one could ever get the full gist of what we said. As an added precaution, we inserted phrases, once-upon-a-times, to make it sound like we were remembering fairy tales, silly stories told to us as little girls. If any of the six or seven other women lying in our bunk elbowed us and told us to shut up, we would fall silent and go to sleep. The next morning, in the few minutes we had before being rushed outside into the icy blackness, we would resume our conversation.

It was not long before we hit upon a scheme, something I proposed merely as a joke. J. clasped my arm in excitement; it was no joke for her. She said we really could make two enormous box kites and transport ourselves over the high electric fences to freedom. It was absurd, but she was so enthusiastic that I went along with her. It was something to dream about, a reason not to die in the godless dark of morning roll call.

We agreed that I would gather the sticks, and she would obtain everything else we needed. As for the design, J. claimed she had a photographic memory. Her uncle was a draftsman who had designed all sorts of things for the German army back in 1915 and 1916. One time, just for fun, he made a box kite for her in her family's living room when she was nine years old. When it was ready, the two of them had taken it to a field; there was too much wind, and the string slipped from J.'s small hands and it disappeared into the mottled clouds of an April afternoon. J. told me she had cried and her uncle had been angry with her. She told me also that the look of the thing, each stage of the design, remained vivid in her memory.

As for me, I had grown up with the diamond-shaped kind. When I was little, my mother would take me on sharp spring days to the square near my father's office, and we would wait until the wind was just right and then launch the kite together. My mother always exclaimed with delight when it took off, for she loved birds and windup toys and all fanciful things. Sometimes my father called out to us from his window or came down to join us before going off to teach a class. So I, too, had memories, though I had never held or seen in person the kind of large box kite we planned to make. Still, photographs of them were not uncommon, and I was fascinated by what my father had told me the Germans had done with them. I had also read about how they were used to record facts about the weather and how, long ago, the Chinese measured distance with them. I had thought about the proportions and painted them in bright colors during my art class.

J. said our box kite could not be in the colors I loved, and I agreed. In my dreams, however, I painted it to look like a spring morning in Kraków: soft blues and pale greens, flecked with yellow light and white blossoms.

J. spent her days in a stuffy room with other women prisoners making and mending uniforms. Sometimes their guard, a pock-faced creature named Descher, went off to drink or use the latrine. The room was always locked so there was no chance of escape. If any of the women had dared break one of the two small windows, one of the guards patrolling outside would have shot her on sight.

Descher's absences, which were growing longer and more frequent, were a blessing. J. took the opportunity to drop things on the floor and slip them up her sleeve or into her shoes. She was not alone in doing such things. All the women took needles and thread and scraps of cloth, sometimes not even bothering to conceal what they were doing if Descher had stepped out or nodded off in a drunken stupor. Later on, in the near dark of the barracks they would patch their ragged clothes or hurriedly stitch an undershirt.

Over a period of several weeks J. acquired a pair of very sharp scissors, a rusty but serviceable darning needle, and a piece of linen, the size of a large dinner napkin. She fretted mightily over the lack of large pieces of fabric and line, which had to be stronger than ordinary string. The cloth she had stolen was just a token, not what we really needed.

In the meantime, I dug a hole in the snow behind the latrine building. The building was a horrible place with a row of holes and a trough down the center aisle. Below that room was an oozing, nauseating nightmare. Along with a bunch of other prisoners, it was my job to shovel out the crawl space. Day after day, I came close to fainting from the stench and horror. Piles of feces and rivers of urine, buzzing flies and scuttling, hissing rats—this was my world. Above me, I heard yelling, swearing guards and screaming, collapsing prisoners. Sometimes there was a crack of gunshot and then wailing, the sound of women sobbing, and more swearing and yelling. And yet there was warmth in that crawl space; I wouldn't freeze to death. So long as I didn't fall facedown in the muck and take ill, I was more or less out of harm's way. I knew I should be grateful for that, and I tried to be.

With the shovel I used on the job, I dug deep in the snow just behind the building, which was surrounded by woods. It was so often snowing, so often dark. No one would know I was here. In the hole I stored the things that J. gave me along with the sticks I gathered. There was little time to distinguish between sticks that were the perfect size and those that were too thick or too flimsy. I just threw in the ones that seemed about the right length, covered over everything with the cloth J. had stolen, and piled on leaves and snow.

J. had started coughing and I was terrified she might have pneumonia. Whenever I could, I gave my soup to her. It was a noxious turnip brew, but it was all I had to give, and perhaps it helped keep my friend alive.

"You've got to hang on," I said to her one morning in the frigid darkness of roll call as she shivered uncontrollably beside me.

"*Wir haben kein Tuch,*" she said between coughs. *We have no cloth.*

The kapo I especially loathed, a pig-faced woman called Lerner, came down our row yelling and scowling and slapping a truncheon against her fat leg. She stopped in front of J. and me. Out of the corner of my eye, I saw J. staring defiantly at Lerner. Her coughing had momentarily stopped. I placed my hand on her back to keep her steady.

"*Fast tot,*" Lerner said, looking her up and down. *Almost dead.*

She kicked J. in the shin. When J. staggered and cried out in pain, I caught her and propped her back up. That made Lerner look at me. "*Lesben,*" she said, her lip curling. A flashing presentiment told me what she was going to do next and I jerked my head to the side. A big glob of her phlegm landed in the snow instead of on my face. I thought she would club me, but instead she shoved me to the ground.

With one glance, Lerner had figured out what I was, though of course she could not know my story. She could not know about the time my beautiful young teacher with slanting green eyes, a woman I had dreamed about night after night, found me alone in the cloakroom at the art league and kissed me long and soundly on the mouth.

Even now, I can conjure the shape and texture of her lips on mine. I was ecstatic that first time. From then on, we met in secret whenever we could, sometimes right during class, in the supply room when the other students were busy at their easels. But often she barely paid me any attention for the two hours I tried to paint a vase of flowers or some such object. Then she would come up behind me after everyone else had left, put her arms around me, and kiss the back of my neck. The janitor who cleaned the floors was unreasonably prompt, so we never had more than a few minutes to ourselves. One Saturday evening, unable to stand it any longer, I slipped out of the house and went to her apartment. She said I should not have come; my parents would be worried to death; she had no telephone to call and tell them I was safe; it was an impossible situation. But even as she was saying those things, she was unbuttoning my coat and pulling me close.

When I got home the next day, I didn't explain myself to my parents, who both looked very pale. They had heard me talk often about my teacher. I had no boyfriends. Seeing that I was fine—actually much more than fine—they must have guessed I had been with her. They told me not to go out again at night. It was too dangerous for a young woman, Jew or gentile. Too dangerous for anyone. I could be jailed, and who knew what would happen to me then.

In the end I didn't have to defy them. The following Monday, I discovered that the art league was boarded up, shut down, and my teacher was nowhere to be found.

So yes, *ich war lesbisch*. But J. was not. She had spoken of a boy she loved, a college student with political interests. He had disappeared long ago. A letter from him had somehow reached her, and she carried it with her always.

After Lerner walked off, I rose to my feet with J.'s help. She brushed the snow off my back and told me our luck would change. Clearly it had just changed for the worse: we had been seen. Until that day I had felt invisible to all except J. The kapos, the officers, even our fellow prisoners, paid me no mind. It was nearly the same for J., though one old woman, a prisoner, had consoled her when her parents were killed and brought her a blanket when she was ill. That woman was dead now.

Two days later, I saw a man I knew from Kraków, a piano tuner who used to come to our house every six months or so when I was a little girl. Mr. W. was an unusually tall man with a cap of graying brown hair and distinctive steel glasses. He used to let me watch as he replaced broken strings and tuned our piano so that it sounded like an instrument made in heaven.

On this day, he was part of a crowd of people who had just disembarked from a screeching, smoking train. There was as always a great deal of confusion and yelling. Somehow I spotted him and without thinking began working my way through the noisy mass to his side. He was looking all around and didn't notice me until I addressed him by name and tugged on the long scarf wrapped around his neck. At first he didn't recognize me. But when I said my name, he touched my cheek and said a few kind words. Unlike most people arriving, he seemed to know exactly what was happening and what fate awaited him.

While the kapos screamed at the crowd, we began being pushed forward in a wave of bodies. Up ahead we could see guards stripping the arrivals of their coats and suitcases. A truck nearby was piled up with these things. Without another word, Mr. W. hoisted me up high and tossed me out of the crowd and into a bank of snow. Then he threw his suitcase and scarf in my direction. In the midst of the tumult, no guard took notice as I grabbed up these items and ran toward the latrine building, a good distance away. With a last look over my shoulder at the truck pushing behind the departing crowd, I hurried behind the trees.

In the shadowed corner where I stored J.'s and my supplies, I looked around again. The stench of the building was so great that no one lingered there, and the tall trees and thick bushes provided cover. Nobody was watching, though I could hear the usual screaming and yelling from inside the latrine. I wrapped Mr. W.'s scarf around the lower half of my face and my neck and tucked the ends inside the blouse I had been made to wear ever since the day I arrived from Kraków. Then I pried open the suitcase. It took some doing because my hands were numb with cold.

I could hardly believe what I found inside: three coils of piano wire, a wire cutter, a pair of work gloves, a wool cap, a small pouch filled with raisins, and a silver flask. I untied the string on the pouch, about the size of my fist, and ate a few raisins. They were stale, but that hardly mattered. With shaking fingers I opened the flask and inhaled the aroma of brandy, something my parents used to drink. A single swallow warmed my insides. I put on the gloves and buried the suitcase while withholding the raisins and wool cap. There was no point in carrying the flask because I knew it would be stolen from me. I placed the pouch of raisins inside the cap and put it on my head.

That night in our bunk, I gave the scarf and one glove to J. I was pleased that she accepted the gifts, which she in her trembling thinness needed so desperately. We ate some raisins and didn't chance our usual whispering.

The next morning, I had a few minutes to tell her about my meeting with Mr. W. before he was pushed forward in the crowd. I felt sure he had been gassed to death. As we gulped down the usual terrible coffee with crusts of bread, J.'s eyes grew wide when I told her about the piano wire and wire cutters. It turned out that she, too, had important news: a large piece of parachute cloth had arrived in the mending room. It had been wrapped around a bundle of soldiers' uniforms and had no apparent utility beyond that. When Descher wandered off, J. emboldened herself to ask the other women if they minded if she took the cloth. They said fine, but they would report her if Descher or anyone else discovered the theft and demanded an explanation. That was all the support she could hope for. She had folded up the cloth and slipped the cumbersome bundle under the back of her blouse.

The fog was heavy that morning and we managed to slip unseen behind some trees. I took the cloth from her and stuck it under my clothes. There was just enough time for me to bury it in my snow pile before I began my workday beneath the latrine.

Finally, it seemed, our luck had changed for the better. In fog so thick we could barely see one another, we slipped away after evening roll call just one night later. Grabbing J.'s hand, I ran with her through the swirling darkness. Even the lights outside the latrine building barely pierced the night. My shovel was propped in the tree-shrouded corner where I had left it, and I dug into the snow pile with furious haste. The suitcase and sticks were still there, and I opened the case and grabbed up the things I had told J. about. But of course there was not enough light to work by. I leaned against J. in the utter discouragement I had known would come sooner or later.

With an exhalation of impatience, she pulled the suitcase away from me and began rummaging around inside it. It was as if she knew what she would find, and I gasped when suddenly her face was illumined in the flare of a match. She had discovered not just a box of matches but also four short, squat candles. These things were in a compartment I had overlooked.

She let out a small cry of excitement and passed one more item from her bare hand to my gloved one. When I saw that it was a compass, I had to stifle the amazed laughter that rose in my throat.

Although we were in a very secluded spot, we piled a wall of snow around us and knelt on the ground while we worked. For hours, when I wasn't involved in some task of my own, I held up one candle after another as J. cut the parachute cloth into strips and stitched them into place with piano wire. She made do with the best of the sticks I had gathered, and it was my job to cut them to the lengths she specified. I worried that we needed glue or twine to hold the wooden frame together, but she told me how to cut notches in the branches so that everything fit together properly. I saw that she was making not one but two box kites and though that slowed her progress, I said nothing. I realized she had a plan, a very definite one, beyond what we had discussed. All of her movements were deliberate, and she rarely spoke except to give me directions.

I ate raisins as we worked, but J. didn't want any. We each had a drink of brandy, just enough to warm ourselves. She said it was important to stay clearheaded so we could finish what we had begun.

By now I was fully aware that J. was a rare individual, not just a girl I had sworn to myself I would help and protect as best I could. Yes, she had a photographic memory and a mechanical aptitude that went far beyond my imagining: these were great gifts. But now that she was finally doing what for weeks she had been seriously plotting while I had been more or less pretending, I divined a determination in her that awed and intimidated me. I would like to say she was a genius, but that barely captures the essence of who or what she was.

Though neither of us had a watch, we both knew when our time had nearly run out. It was still night but the weather had changed. The fog had given way to stars and a stiff, strong wind. This was all to the good, J. murmured more to herself than to me.

"Du bist fast bereit," J. suddenly said. *You are almost ready.* She stood up and wiped snow from her skirt. Then she laid the flask, raisins, wire cutters, compass, matches, and remaining candle inside the piece of cloth she had stolen weeks ago. With a length of wire, she quickly transformed it into a pouch and knotted one end of the wire around my wrist.

My heart began beating like wild. Anyone reading this will wonder how I had not foreseen this moment when one of us would attempt to escape while the other remained behind. But as I said, I had not thought we would get to this point. It was J., only J., who believed what we were doing was real.

She gave me back the scarf and glove. There was no time or proper material to make a seat, she said, so I would have to position myself between the two kites as best I could, with my hands firmly gripping the wires. When my protests rose above a whisper, she shushed me and squeezed my gloved hands around the wires extending from the kites to the two coils of wire on the ground. She picked up those coils, backed away, and told me to let the wind do its work.

I darted toward her, my hands still wrapped around the wires, and told her I couldn't go, not without her. In the starlight

I could see tears on her cheeks. *"Du mußt versuchen,"* she said. *You must try.*

With that she backed away from me and began running the length of the latrine building. In a moment the wires grew taut and to my astonishment my feet began to leave the snowy ground. The wind was strong and steady. The parachute cloth and the sticks held fast, and soon I was rising high above the electric fence surrounding the camp. The nearest watchtower was at some distance, and its spotlight pointed toward the ground, not the sky.

J.'s shadowy outline quickly vanished, yet the tension of the wires bound me to her. The wind stung my eyes as I cried out her name. My feet dangled in the darkness and my arms began to ache, but I would not, could not, let go. An unearthly exhilaration filled me as I rose ever higher and the stars kissed my hair and I let the wind do its work as J. told me I must.

In ten minutes—or an hour, I could not say—I would land with surprising softness in a distant field. Mr. W.'s compass would lead me back to Kraków and on to a series of hiding places and then to a large ship and a new life, quite a long one, on the Lower East Side of Manhattan. It was there I would spend my days painting rectangles and diamonds against backgrounds of blue and black and starry violet. I would find a lover whose long hair I would plait in a golden braid. She would hold me while I wept for the girl who knew exactly when to let go. On winter nights, with moonlight pouring in the window, I would stare for hours at the ceiling above our bed and wonder whether it was J. or I who had the rare gift of invention. Which one of us, really, had found the way?

BUS TRIP, AUCKLAND - OTAKI, 2014, WINDOW SEAT

Charlotte Marie Chadwick

buttercups sprinkle up like quotation marks

between darker clumps of green &

adolescent sheep clotted with milk

sink their spindly roots into the dirt & suck

one last sweet drop from

once-bush burnt to ash

a century ago morning cloud

clings to the bare flesh rolls

of unscrubbed repetitious hills

my counting wanders from the track

a bright cluck trill of a tui

cuts right through but the air closes

back around it

like an upside down lake

like the song were a stone thrown upward

and those tiny mounds of ripples will fade

my counting does not bring sleep

here things happen too soon

tipped with yolk sunrise

fledgings don't last long

holding onto my breath and the image of a paper plane in the cold

watching it circle three times

widdershins

before falling to land

beyond the lumpish slab agreeing against my ribcage

beneath the sound of the skeleton grin that echoes inside my head

COLONIAL ACRES

Brandy T. Wilson

Sugar was tipsy and gay. And Barbara was already grinning and rosy cheeked, which, Sugar knew, meant that she was as high as she could get. They were both in new Spring outfits, had new haircuts, and it was Thursday—payday. They were at their favorite restaurant bar, Sleet & Cannon, the only one in Mid-town that still allowed smoking. Sugar lit up a cigarette—she'd lost count at how many she'd had—and offered one to Barbara.

"No thanks. I think I'll hold off for a while," Barbara said and waved the pack away.

Sugar lit her cigarette. "More for me." She laughed as she exhaled the smoke over their heads, though she couldn't help but feel like some kind of drug pusher. "What? Are you on a kick again, Barb? You know that shit doesn't work *while* you're drinking."

"No. I'm not. I- I just have something else on my mind."

Sugar was afraid to ask so she flagged the waitress down instead and ordered another round, which Barbara waved off as well. As soon as the waitress left Sugar's drink on the table and walked away, Barbara was out of her seat and kneeling down on one knee on the dirty bar floor in front of Sugar.

Sugar froze. She knew exactly what was about to happen and wished to God Barbara had not chosen to do it *here*, in *public*, at a *bar*. But here it was and Barbara gave a sweet heartfelt and quickly-rendered proposal, and there was the ring, the very ring that Sugar had pointed at in that catalogue that happened to come in the mail, and that they had happened to peruse during one of their "what if" conversations. All told, Sugar knew it was coming. She didn't know when or how, but she knew, and she knew she'd say yes. She had to.

Four months later, the grass was patchy at best in front of their new suburban, East Memphis home. The house was on

Brook Falls Lane, but there was no brook—or any kind of natural water source—within thirty miles. Sugar had fertilized the yard months ago, but somewhere between the Fourth of July and Labor Day, she had let it go. With the heat and the water bill, she just didn't want to deal with it. It was enough to mow the damn thing every week. Now big oblong sections were thinned by weeds and yellowed grass. It made the whole yard look dead, which in turn made the house look run down, shabby and worse than their neighbors' houses.

She pulled her satchel out of the trunk and looped the strap over her head. Her heels sunk in the sod before she made it to the weedy cracked sidewalk leading up to the front door. Even the shrubs she'd put in in May were fading, looking pitiful and forlorn. She tried to ignore it all as she dug out her keys.

She hated the suburbs anyway. She had better things to do, she told herself, than pamper grass and flowerbeds. Barbara, who'd wanted to move away as soon as they signed the papers, agreed, even though it had all been Barbara's idea in the first place: to get married, join their finances, buy a house in the suburbs, settle down, grow up. All so they could have a baby. The baby was both of their ideas.

But Sugar was always restless. She drank too much when she could, never bothered to keep her bank account in line, and ate like a teenager. She was always surprised when she didn't gain weight after her binges. But she didn't, though she was sure afraid she might start, settled in nice and tight like she was out East with the sparse lots and large TVs. And as a lesbian, this was certainly not the life she'd imagined.

Down at Sun's Harvest Food co-op, Jo, one of the only other lesbians they knew in town, had rolled her eyes when they told her about the house out East. "We're different, special. If we up and assimilate into what *they* think is the be-all-end-all of everything, marriage and two and a half children in the suburbs, then who are we anymore?" Jo insisted on explaining their reluctance to settle in, or settle rather, as she put out the organic peas. "I am a lesbian, well because I love women, but also because I'm different. I don't need to fit in to anyone else's notion of life. Even before I knew what attraction was, I knew I was different. I plan to stay that way." They'd met Jo a few years ago at a bar when they still went out every weekend to the drag show and the dance club, when they still lived in Midtown along with the rich gay men, the struggling lesbians, and the hipsters.

"It's inside the loop—in the city," Barbara added, almost like an apology.

"Might as well still be the suburbs." Jo lifted a crate up to her shoulder, nodded, and

walked to the back. Sugar and Barbara stared at Jo as she left. She was not really attractive so much as appealing. She had that rugged look of a lesbian who works outside all day, but it looked good on her, sexy lines about the eyes, just-right-fitting, worn-out jeans hugging her curves, strong arms, work-glove-covered hands. Sugar felt both envious and desirous. She could never decide which one won out.

When Jo turned the corner at the end of the aisle, Barbara sucked in her breath and stood up noticeably straighter, which left a sinking feeling in Sugar's gut. Sugar and Barbara finished their shopping with little conversation. In line, the woman in front of them lugged her giggling, plump baby from one hip to the next and they squeezed each other's hands. Sugar thought she could literally feel a tug in her ovaries.

Sugar put her satchel in the oversized chair in the living room. She carried everything, her sheers, her new clippers, her best flat iron in every day, afraid to leave it at work. The last time she'd left it, the salon had closed down, locked her stuff up away from her, and she'd lost everything, along with her clients. She was always threatening to open her own salon, but she knew the overhead would eat her profits and she made good money at the new place, had a good set of regulars, and there was always a steady stream of walk ins. She was a popular choice because she'd refused to let her wild hair go, still wearing it shaved up one side, high and lowlighted at the top, and usually a different color every month or so streaking the rest.

"Barb, I'm home!" Sugar yelled and waited a beat for her kiss, their daily ritual, with a sigh.

"Out here, baby," Barb yelled from the back patio, a smile in her voice.

Barb's shoulder-length hair was tied back in a low ponytail, and she had her golfing cap on and those god-awful sunglasses with the strap that kept them on her head. Sugar always thought Barb should have been doing outdoorsy work instead of answering phones, taking orders, and dispatching the dirt for the construction guys she worked for. But she was the office manager, accounts manager, and supervisor now. She was settled in nice and tight. Sugar laughed as she slunk out the back door, attempting to elude the new kitten that got out anyway.

"What's so funny?"

"Nothing," Sugar pulled her in and kissed her and then tugged at the strap on Barbara's glasses.

"How was the *salon*?" Barb, as she'd told Sugar many times, grew up calling it a beauty shop and thought salon was pretentious.

"Good. I think I snagged a new client today." Sugar hated relating the daily grind with Barb.

"That's great, hon!"

"How was your day?" Sugar surprised even herself with her enthusiasm.

"Fine, fine," Barb said and got up to open the grill lid. "I got us some wine. Will you open it?"

Sugar went inside and pulled the crisp, white wine, her favorite, from the fridge and poured two glasses. "What's the occasion?"

Barb just raised an eyebrow as she flipped the chicken on the grill. "Sit down, relax."

"It smells good, baby. Thank you for cooking."

After dinner, they were quiet, and Barb fidgeted with a string on her chair, and then picked up the kitten and put him in her lap, petting him gently, cooing at him like a baby. The kitten had, after all, been their attempt to satisfy their baby cravings, if just for a little while. Sugar had little patience for him, but he was cute. Half the time she couldn't remember his name. Tom, was it? Or Tomboy?

"So, are you going to tell me what's up or am I going to have to pry it out of you?"

"Did you smoke today?" Tomboy stood on Barb's lap and meowed loudly as if demanding an answer too.

Sugar blushed. She hated getting caught and felt the heat rise in her. She had washed her hands, brushed her teeth, even sprayed a little perfume in her hair. How could she still smell it? "Just one."

"Sugar."

"Okay, but I didn't buy a pack," she lied. There was, right that second, a pack in her car, and she was a terrible liar. She knew Barb knew.

"We talked about this. You said you'd quit two months before the wedding so that we could try for a baby right after."

"I know. I know."

"We only have a month and a half until the ceremony, baby. Do you not want to do it?"

"What, have a baby? How could you even ask that? Of course I do." She almost felt the tug every time the word "baby" was spoken.

"No, I mean get married."

Sugar's mouth went dry. Did she want to get married? She really didn't know. She wanted to be with Barb. She wanted a baby. She wanted it all, safety and security. She just didn't know if she wanted it all this way. She got up and grabbed Tomboy and put him in her lap. She petted him under the chin and behind the ears, even tried cooing at him but he jumped down anyway and ran back to Barb, twirling around her legs.

"I told you I did, but you know how I feel about marriage. You know how I feel about it all, the whole straight-acting thing."

"Because some old lesbian said its cooler to be disenfranchised, to rebel? Haven't you rebelled enough? Isn't it enough that your family barely talks to us, much less accepts us as a couple?"

Sugar did agree with the damned old lesbian, she thought, and she didn't really give a shit that her family didn't talk to them. It was a relief most of the time. But still, it was *her* family. "What does my family have to do with all of this?"

"Nothing. I'm sorry, but you have to quit smoking. It's what we planned baby, and I want you to be around for a long time. I'm scared you are going to up and die on me."

"And you don't want to marry someone who might die?"

"Not right away!" Barb gave a half laugh. "Besides, the damn things are expensive! We have a wedding to pay for, Sugar!"

"I know. I know. I'm keeping track of my money, Barb, I promise." This was always a point of contention, and Barb was certainly the stabilizing factor in Sugar's bank account.

After dinner Barb got up to clear the table. Sugar grabbed the grill brush and scraped at the rack. She lifted it with the oven mitt and then ran it under the faucet outside, one of the many conveniences she did love about their new home.

"Do you have any more?" Barb said as she poured them both another glass of wine and sat back down.

Sugar went through the house and to her car to get the pack. Now she was corrupting them both, and she could feel her chest grow heavier as she walked. Before this pack it had been two whole weeks since they'd smoked. She took out two cigarettes and threw the pack in the outside trashcan. The last one, she told herself.

After Barb went to sleep, Sugar downed the last of the bottle of wine and then dug out the whiskey. Well lit by this point, she went up to the attic just to gather a few more winter sweaters before it got too cold outside and she spotted the box her mother had sent her years ago. She knelt down and tore the packing tape off the top of the box. On top was a yellow dress trimmed in white lace. She ran her hands along the ruffles at the bottom of the tiny dress, complete with puffy bloomers. She vaguely remembered a picture of herself in that very outfit, and somehow she felt she could picture another baby in it, a daughter, *her* daughter. She was so real, as if she were already there, right there in front of her. She felt so emotional, but she was too drunk to cry.

The next morning, Sugar dug the pack out of the trash. She had to tip it over to get to them and in the process touched something slimy. Afraid she'd wake Barb if she went back in, she dug out an old water bottle in her trunk and a rag and cleaned herself up before getting in her car to drive to work. She smoked the rest of the pack that day before she was off work and swore she wouldn't buy any more. She'd read about a concoction that would clear your system of nicotine faster, in a day instead of two, so she could just get all the withdrawals over with sooner and hopefully get back on track. She stopped by the co-op on the way home and got some dandelion root, lemon, and ginger.

Jo was working produce when she passed by. She nodded. "How's married life treatin' ya?"

Sugar smiled. "We aren't married yet." Immediately she wished she was.

Jo gave her a wicked grin and turned back to the broccoli in her hands.

Sugar felt something in her gut then and she turned and almost ran to the supplements aisle. When she'd found what she needed and checked out, she shuffled past the produce without looking up.

She wanted a cigarette when she got to her car so badly she thought she might gnaw off her arm. She felt under the seat, nothing. She took a deep breath and started the car. As she was pulling out of the parking lot, she saw Jo step out back and put a cigarette to her lips. Just then a car horn blew behind her. Jo caught her stare, but Sugar ducked her head and drove on.

In the cool of the living room, Barb was wild eyed and surrounded by magazines, sample invitations, and pictures of cakes. She leapt up off the couch, seeming surprised, when Sugar walked in. "You've come to rescue me!" She shuffled through papers and threw her arms around Sugar before she even had the chance to put her satchel down. She kissed her hard, pushing her tongue through her lips. "Good job, baby. I'm proud of you."

Sugar leaned back, "Why?"

"You didn't smoke today," she said, smiling. "Did you?"

"No! How you going to say you are proud of me and then accuse me?" Sugar unwrapped Barbs arms and put her satchel down, sitting with it into the chair away from Barb so she wouldn't smell the cigarettes she'd somehow missed.

Barb just stood there, her arms limp at her sides, in the middle of the living room.

"What the hell is all of this?" Sugar leaned forward and flipped through the mess.

"Nothing. You won't be interested." Barb went to the back of the house.

"Come on, come back. I am interested. Is it for the wedding?" Barb had gone to the bedroom, she knew. She was going to go to bed—her favorite thing to do to Sugar. When Sugar had the next day off and they could be together, hang out late and sleep in together, Barb would let one little thing piss her off and go take a nap that would turn into going to bed for the night, or at least until after Sugar had given up and gone to bed herself.

Sugar could see Jo, dragging on a cigarette—could feel Jo against her. She imagined what it would be like to take Jo to a bar. Sugar went down the hall and took off her shoes, undressed and slipped in bed beside Barb. "Come on, baby. It's only 8:30."

"Did you get the cleanse stuff?"

"Yes, that's why I'm late. I told you I would. I want this, all of this, with you." She nuzzled into Barb's neck and was grateful when she didn't pull away. When they made love that night, Barb said "thank you." And though it was in the throes of an orgasm, somehow, Sugar knew it wasn't for the sex—she'd never thanked Sugar for that.

Barb left before Sugar the next Monday morning and Sugar resisted every urge she had to get up and go to the store to get cigarettes, even though she'd figured she could get them, smoke, and then shower. She knew Barb would never know, but she resisted. And she kept on resisting that whole week, through the color swatches, through the picking of invitations, through the guest list. She even began getting a little excited, especially when it came to the clothes, the cute little white frock with the pink accents she'd found at a second-hand shop and the tailored suit Barb had been talking about for months. They were almost done with the planning and they'd only begun a couple of months earlier.

It was going to be a quickie wedding with just a few friends, a destination wedding they'd started planning as soon as they found out that New York had legalized same-sex marriage. Sugar's brother lived there now and they'd have it at his loft, right by the park. No other family would be there, they knew, so it was nice that Sugar's brother offered his place.

"Did you send the e-vites today?" Barb asked as they parked at the co-op.

Rage shot through Sugar. "Of course I did! Why do you think I am so incompetent? You have second-guessed every single little thing I've done for this wedding. I do not need to be micromanaged like the dimwitted secretaries your boss hires!"

"I am not trying to—I know you aren't dimwitted, Sugar, or incompetent! I-I just know you aren't really all that thrilled about this wedding."

"For the hundredth time, Barb, I am! I want to marry you! I do take this seriously! Sometimes, I think I am more serious about it than you are!" She said, though she knew she didn't think this at all. Just a jab, she thought.

Barb's eyes were watery as she looked at Sugar. She was obviously hurt, and something else. "I'm sorry. I know you are. It's just so stressful."

"See—"

"No, don't! I do not want to be reminded that you have gone through this before! I know you told me so, but it isn't going to be like your last wedding, right? Right?"

Just as Sugar leaned in to take the keys out of the ignition, Jo stepped out back for a smoke. She put it to her mouth, lit it, and leaned back against the brick building to take in a long drag. Sugar couldn't stop staring at her.

"Right. I'm sorry too. Let's just go get something for dinner tonight. We can shop tomorrow."

Barb was fully crying now.

Sugar unbuckled her seat belt and pulled Barb to her. "Don't cry, baby. It will be fine. We are both just stressed. I'm sorry. I want you. I want to marry you and for us to have babies, a family, just like we planned."

Barb pulled away from her and cried into her hands. "Don't placate me, Sugar!"

"It isn't—this isn't anything like my first one, baby. What the hell did I know
about anything then?"

"You knew you didn't want to be married."

Sugar didn't have an answer to that. She just started the car and tried not to look at Jo as she pulled away, driving home instead of stopping for food.

Barb cried all the way home.

Sugar had only been twenty-two when she married the first time. Too young. That was always what she told people, that she was too young and didn't even know herself yet, hadn't even admitted to herself that she was a lesbian. She'd married a boy she'd fell in with when she was working on flunking out of college, which she did the very next year. He was a sweet boy and loved her, would have stayed with her forever, she knew, would have done anything she wanted to. Two years later she met her first girlfriend and was gone before she knew what hit her. The boy had understood, had understood everything and let her go. She broke his heart to pieces, but he let her go. And then the girl broke hers.

She was full of guilt and shame but when she'd left that marriage she'd left the whole idea of it behind, saying she'd never marry again. She wanted to be in a lesbian village, not a marriage, she'd always said. But then she met Barb. And Sugar had always wanted children. And then they moved here to this rough southern city and bought a house in a good part of town. And here they were. Getting married in two weeks, a party for them in one week. And there was Jo. She wanted to flog herself. She wanted a cigarette. She wanted a drink. She wanted to run to Midtown.

She put Barb to bed, crying on an empty stomach, and went to get some fast food—something else they vowed to stop doing. She figured it was better than buying a pack of cigarettes and a bottle of wine. She passed by the co-op on the way home, greasy fries in her lap. Jo wasn't outside. She wondered what kind of car Jo drove—a truck, she imagined. She wondered what Jo did when she wasn't at the co-op. She knew Jo lived in Midtown, in a little house surrounded by a bunch of other lesbians, or so she imagined, that village Sugar always fantasized about. Or she imagined that it was surrounded by hipsters that Jo sneered at every day as she made out with girls on her front porch—Sugar had seen that in a movie once. And then Sugar imagined it had been her that Jo put her lips around instead of that cigarette.

Barb was on the porch in the dying sunlight when she drove up. Luckily she'd at least thought to get Barb a hamburger and fries, though she didn't know if Barb would take it. She was more determined than Sugar was. Always had been. Sugar would have to apologize for getting them off their diet. Sugar always had to apologize.

When she got out of the car, Barb stood up. She had a pack of cigarettes in her hand. Sugar's heart thumped and she searched her memory. Had she forgotten a hidden pack? Had she left the ones in the trash from a couple of weeks ago? She was about to tell her, again, that she hadn't been smoking, but Barb took one out of the pack, and Sugar saw that it was brand new. Barb lit it. "I have to tell you—" she started.

"What? That you're smoking? I can see that."

"No." Barb sat on the bench on the front porch and put her face in her hands and then wiped her eyes. "I'm sorry." There was a bag beside her on the porch, just out of view until Sugar was right up on it.

"What is this? What's wrong, Barb? It was just a little fight. We fight all the time. Couples fight. We work through it. That's how it works."

"I am so sick of you telling me how things work—as if—as if—" Barb took a drag off the cigarette and blew it out with force. "Oh hell, who cares. You're right—you were right about it all, the wedding, moving out here, everything, and I'm leaving you, Sugar. I don't know if it's forever, but it's for now. I can't do *this* right now."

Just then an old Buick pulled up to the curb in front of the house. It looked like something Sugar's grandmother would have driven in the 80s. It was gold, or champagne, rather, and the seats squeaked when the driver got out. It was Jo. She got out, a cigarette dangling from her lips, and nodded at Sugar. She was still wearing her co-op T-shirt and worn out jeans. She went around and opened the trunk.

"I called her when I got home and she agreed to let me stay at her house for a few days," Barb said, but there was something—something not right, not truthful in her tone, Sugar knew. Before Sugar could say a word, Barb had walked across the patchy lawn and put her bag in Jo's trunk. "I'll come back next week while you're at work to get my stuff. We'll figure out the rest then." And then she was gone, her and Jo in the front seat of a worn-out old

Buick, a trail of smoke streaming out of the cracked passenger side window. She hadn't even left Sugar a cigarette.

As the sound of the car faded, the kitten popped up into the window seal and sat down, blinking at Sugar. Sugar dug her keys out of her pocket, "I'll be right back, baby," she said, and touched the screen while the kitten rubbed his face on the glass.

Swirling her engagement ring on her finger, Sugar got in her car and drove towards Midtown. It was Thursday night. She needed a smoke. And maybe a little wine.

TAROT AND MASTURBATION

Rae Liberto

I pull the strength card.
A lion with a rose in her mouth:

Mastery of Emotions.

I wash my vibrator
in hypoallergenic soap.

I wish there was leave-in
conditioner for the heart.

You leave me a dry
tangled feeling.

My new crush paints me pictures of her breasts
I hang them like trophies.

I lost you.
But I am still a winner.

VESTALIA

Megan Tierney

Kathleen-the-Astronaut is how Kat's mother introduced her at parties. Her mother was so proud of her and all her accomplishments, which only made Kat wonder why she was only Kathleen-the-Astronaut, why not Kathleen-the-Engineer, or even Doctor-Kathleen-Barnes. Kathleen-the-Astronaut fell flat on its ass, considering the extraorbital community Kat's mother and all their friends, family, and peers lived in technically made them *all* astronauts. Kat, however, worked on terraforming projects, as well as the occasional exploratory mission, which somehow made her distinctive in her mother's eyes, though that was often how mothers thought regardless of their child's profession.

Kat's fingers stretched out like the legs of spiders, long and spindly. Her job required steadiness, sureness, and precision, and Kat's large hands were good at what they did. Kat's days were filled with tinkering and fixing and building, which left the skin hard, with little give. The pads of her fingers matched those of a dog's paws, toughened from constant use, pliant underneath. Those long, strong fingers were gifts received from her father, among others including, but not limited to, her proclivity for helping others, her temper, and the shape of her nose.

Some of these gifts she liked, others she did not. She recognized the constant heartache she endured precipitated from putting too much into her interpersonal relationships. It seemed to Kat that she was giving away every piece of herself, throwing her entire heart and mind into her friends' and relatives' problems, and yet she always found more to give away.

She would turn her face this way and that in the mirror, checking to see which angle best hid the long slope of her nose and the large, dark nostrils. Kat sometimes caught herself tilting her head down and slightly to the side, enough to ensure the nearest shuttle camera was recording her good side. This occurred only in transient times, mostly when Kat had spent the morning on the phone with one of her parents, or after a particularly bad date. Otherwise, Kat liked to pretend her nose didn't exist at all, that such a large protrusion did not in fact mar a perfectly good face, in her own opinion. She quite liked everything else, the medium skin, the clear eyes, high cheekbones, and even her lips, which weren't quite symmetrical, but she liked them well enough anyway.

One of the community's councils for Interpersonal Preservation and Procreation (commonly abbreviated IPAP) approached Kat a few times in effort to encourage her to, if she wouldn't get married and have children herself, donate her eggs. She was reasonably good looking and intelligent, qualities often desired by prospective infertile mothers who went through IPAP to have children, as well as sought after by colonial subcommittees representing all reaches of their current star system. Kat was not alone in this recruitment of sorts, most of her coworkers had been likewise approached at various times, even the married ones, to donate to the cause. Kat's commander had donated eggs various times, even at her advanced age. Commander Ryanne Cavanaugh reasoned that she wouldn't be having any more kids anyway, since her youngest was nearing eighteen, and if she sent some eggs off to the edge of the system, it was unlikely the genetic lines would cross soon enough to cause any genetic failures or birth defects. Kat wasn't sure she agreed, imagining her eggs, her hypothetical future children on a ship to who-knows-where to be raised by who-knows-who. It felt strange. *Hi, mom*, she imagined one of these hypothetical future children appearing at her door. Then she imagined ten. Then twenty. Fifty.

Commander Cavanaugh reminded Kat about their lives, the very work they did brought life to a young star system, and humanity's best chance for survival lay in creating the most offspring for the most chance to survive. Genetic advantages, at that. Kat nodded thoughtfully when the commander gave her the impromptu lesson, though she remembered much of it from her studies in pursuit of her PhD. She still didn't quite agree. She fully supported the commander's donations to science and humanity in the form of genetic material, in fact, Kat couldn't think of another person more suited to help populate new civilizations. Ryanne Cavanaugh's eldest four children, the ones she made with her husband and reared herself, at least between off-station missions, excelled in their studies. The youngest child already received recruitment letters for military training, though she had not yet finished high school.

Kat and the commander's firstborn, Jordan, spent a year in the same class rotation for postgraduate study, and developed a deep friendship, and then a relationship cut short the minute Kat was drafted into Ryanne Cavanaugh's Vesta mission team. Vesta's thirty-year schedule ensured a close relationship with mother as well as daughter.

Jordan, without saying much to Kat (though Kat had her hunches and suspicions), drifted away. Kat found out a few years later that Jordan secured a place with the Janus mission team, as their botanist and biologist.

Vesta's botanist, Ariadne Jane "AJ" Dawson, existed in direct contrast to Jordan. Where Jordan was quiet and soft, AJ was loud and harsh. When Jordan was up late at night studying or experimenting, AJ was asleep. Where Jordan was tall and fair, AJ was small and dark. AJ laughed loud and long, and refused to apologize for anything. Perhaps that was why Kat liked AJ so much.

AJ's bottom teeth crowded slightly in the front, rarely hidden by her full lips, something Kat noticed almost immediately upon their meeting, since AJ was always talking or laughing. Practically the only time Kat didn't see them was when she and AJ shared a kiss. AJ was everything Jordan was not, and in that, all Kat could think about was Jordan and how different AJ kissed, how different she felt, and how different she smelled. AJ's moans were Jordan's funeral dirge in Kat's mind, though Kat hadn't meant to cry at all, let alone so much, nor still in AJ's presence. She avoided AJ as much as possible after that, a difficult feat on a small craft built to comfortably accommodate seven crew members.

Kat's job was to make sure the Vesta crew remained on schedule, and that the ship survived the trip. The last four members rounded out the mission, with Captain Brian Soon piloting, geneticist Dr. Paula Suárez working closely with AJ on creating life, and mission specialists Gwendolyn Valentine and Alexei Sopova assisting the rest wherever needed. These were the six people Kat would be spending the majority of the next thirty-year stretch with. A circuitous route from their station all the way to the furthest reaches of the known systems in ever-swelling spirals would allow them to see their family and friends only once in a long while. At least it was better than nothing.

Kat sat in her seat towards the back of the pod that contained Vesta's navigation and controls. Captain Soon and Commander Cavanaugh sat near the main controls, with the other four scattered between them and her. Kat kept her eyes on the readouts on the screen in front of her, her main concern at the moment being the engines. She watched the fuel, pressure, and output readings intently. However, an hour later, Vesta was cruising freely, micro-acceleration steadily increasing their velocity.

Kat took her helmet off when Valentine announced a successful launch. The crew rose, almost as one, stretching their backs and necks before filing out of the command pod. Further back, the Vesta expanded into a more livable space, with a small room for each of them, and slightly larger rooms for socializing, cooking and eating, and of course, conducting experiments. Since travel took up most of their mission time, their work would be dependent on getting much of it done before arriving at target planetoids. As the engineer, once Kat made her rounds, she was to spend her days helping. *Glorified mission specialist,* she complained to AJ during their pre-mission training. Before she slept with AJ. Before she cried *while* sleeping with AJ. *Dr. Mission Specialist*, AJ shot back with that oddly crooked grin she had. *Queen of the mission specialists.*

Now, Kat checked the commander's schedule as she went back to her cubby of a room.

Mission Day 1

Launch +1h

Personal Time: 30 minutes

Daily Assignments: Genetics Phase I: Dr. Suarez, Valentine; Botany Phase I: Dr. Dawson, Dr. Barnes; Chemistry Phase I: Dr. Cavanaugh, Sopova; Inventory/Off: Soon

Meals: +6h and +12h

Daily report to be e-mailed to Commander Cavanaugh before +15h

Well, *fuck*. Kat set her tablet down on the tiny sleeping space and ran a hand through her brown hair to pull it out of the loose bun it had been in under her helmet minutes earlier. The last thing she wanted to do was work with AJ on the botany project. She pulled a sweatshirt emblazoned with the IPAP logo on it over her head and slipped out of her room.

Soon would never trade an inventory day, so she tried Sopova. She stopped at the door marked Sopova, A, and knocked softly. "Sopova? Alex?" Kat said, poking her head inside when she was beckoned.

"Trade with me?" she asked Sopova. Her fingers curled in the sleeves of her sweatshirt, sucking the cuffs inwards into her grip.

Alexei stood up from her bed and rummaged in one of her drawers. "Not likely," she replied with a frown. "Why?" She peeked over her shoulder at Kat.

Kat shrugged. "Come on, I'll trade you one of my inventory days next," she urged. She stared right into Sopova's steel blue eyes. Her face didn't change though, remaining stoic.

"Try Valentine." Kat excused herself and did just that, but met similar resistance. Valentine almost took the offer of an extra inventory day, but eventually refused, for fear of Commander Cavanaugh's displeasure, the very reason Kat didn't tell the commander about her fraternization with AJ. If Kat lost this job, she would have been relegated to some awful civil engineering position back on the station, which mostly entailed new and (not so) exciting ways to dispose of waste.

Kat's personal time ended up mostly wasted asking everyone except the commander and AJ herself to trade spots. Soon laughed right in her face. She knew she shouldn't have bothered. Kat didn't manage to write off more than a couple sentences to her mother by way of mission update before she had to report to the lab to start work. The commander hated deviance from the schedule. They'd learned that early in training.

"Heeeeeeeeey, Kat," AJ called to her, already in the lab by the time Kat resigned herself to her day's fate. Kat smiled in reply, though with so few teeth exposed, it was more of a grimace.

"What's first?" Kat asked, pushing her sleeves up to her elbows.

"First I wanna know why you've been ducking me like a professional limbo dancer."

Kat looked up from washing her hands. Her face was already turning red. "Haven't been," she muttered.

AJ cocked an eyebrow at her from across the lab. "I mean sure it was kinda weird that you cried after we fucked, but... It happens. Never to me before, but you know. Other people." Kat's face stuck itself in a shocked expression as AJ rambled on. "And besides, it's not a big deal, is it? Cavanaugh told me you had a thing with her daughter, so I'm not judging you or anything, but it made me feel less fucking awful. I was worried about performance anxiety after that, but I'm good now."

Kat swallowed a hard lump in her throat and stared at AJ with wide eyes. "Oh my-- AJ, shut up. Let's just get this shit done," she gasped, shaking her head. Her mind raced. Cavanaugh knew about her thing that was a very big, very serious thing, with Jordan? Fuck, fuck, fuck. Kat stalked over to the cabinets and jiggled the door. They, and all the drawers, were specially designed to stay shut in case something hit the ship or otherwise caused it to lurch. This just meant it was a pain in the ass to retrieve anything, especially food.

"So we're good? We're cool?" AJ asked, pulling up the Phase I plans on her tablet and standing it up on the work table.

"We're cool," Kat muttered, face stuck in the cabinet. "What do we need?"

The rotation continued, and Kat only had to see AJ for work detail once or twice per week for the next year. She cherished her "morning" and "evening" systems checks. It was the only time of her day that she actually did her job. Life support systems, check. Waste reclaimer, check. Engines, check. Hull integrity, check. Airlock integrity, check. Telemetry, check. Communications array, check. She went around the Vesta to physically check on filters. It wasn't that she didn't trust the profuse readouts, but that she preferred a more hands on approach. Kat brushed an air filter with her finger. It came up clean. She closed the vent and screwed it back into place. They were approaching their first planetoid, with all Phase I projects complete, they were ready to test them on the potential world. Kat returned to the wall screen to input her signature for Vesta's morning checkup. The ETA to orbit around the first planetoid up in the corner of the screen caught her eye. Three days left. She turned to look out one of the large windows. Kat pressed the intercom button on the bottom of the screen. "Soon? You'd better get up to the control room."

Kat turned to stand at the window. She bit the inside of her cheek and ignored Soon's questions over the intercom and went up to the control room instead. Commander Cavanaugh and Soon joined her. "We're too close to the planetoid," she said in response to their questioning looks. She pointed out the windows. "We're already in orbit. Vesta is going to collide with it if we don't do something."

"Shit," Soon hissed, rushing over to the pilot's chair to double check her findings.

"How did we not notice this?" Cavanaugh said. She hung her head.

"I swear telemetry has been five by five all year," Kat replied. Her teeth gnawed at a small patch of loose skin on her lip.

"Obviously it *hasn't* been. Get everyone up here and strapped in. I'm going to pull us out before we hit atmo," Soon urged.

The commander put in the order as Kat pulled her suit and helmet on. Within minutes, all seven Vesta crew members were buckled into their seats. Immediately, Soon activated reverse thrusters, jerking them back against their headrests. Kat's eyes remained focused on the engines, on the fuel, breathing shakily.

"We're not far enough out," Valentine said. "You can only use 12% more fuel or else we won't make the first round back for resupply," Kat added.

"You have to pull us back a kilometer!" Valentine said, more urgently this time.

"Alright!" Soon snapped through a clenched jaw.

The ship rumbled, protesting Soon's every maneuver. Finally, it roared as the ship hurtled into the upper atmosphere. Kat's eyes watered from the blinding light enveloping the ship.

"If I burn the thrusters to get us back up, we'll be floating helplessly in space," Soon shouted over the roaring.

"Land us safely instead, we'll send out a resupply request," Commander Cavanaugh yelled back.

"It could take years for a probe to get to us," Kat said. The crew fell silent, only the sound of creaking metal, rushing wind, and low rumbling filled Kat's ears while the ship hurtled towards the planet's surface. She stared at her screen, as her crewmates were also doing, as though they could do something to prevent this catastrophic emergency landing. Only Soon actually worked at his station, burning thrusters and adjusting flaps.

A loud crunch added to the metallic din. Kat whirled around to look at Valentine. She squinted to sharpen her focus on Valentine's screen. They'd lost a rudder.

"Ten thousand feet, we're coming in too hot," Kat said.

"I know," Soon said. "I've got one last trick." He pressed a button on his dashboard and the ship jolted. The landing parachute.

"Are you fucking crazy?" Kat screamed. "That's designed for water--" The ship bucked again and continued hurtling down towards the planet surface. AJ had unstrapped herself and gone to a window, not without banging various parts of her body on parts of the cockpit.

"It caught the broken rudder. It's torn," she said. "Strap back in, it's going to be a messy landing," Commander Cavanaugh said.

Kat closed her eyes. Their terminal velocity was too high. They were already at just a few thousand feet and plummeting. The craft would turn to stannic confetti, even if they happened to hit marsh-like conditions at the surface. She thought back to her mother, alone on their home ship. She wondered how it would appear on the news feeds. *Please don't say Kathleen-the-Astronaut,* she pleaded silently. *Dr. Kathleen Barnes, accomplished engineer, is survived by her mother and a small collection of pre-nuclear Earth sculptures.*

Her forehead creased until her eyebrows were almost touching in the center. The crewmates were shouting out numbers and suggestions, but she heard none. Potential obituary reports floated through her mind instead. What would Jordan think? Surely Jordan wouldn't really care about Kat's death when Commander Cavanaugh's would overshadow it. Her mother would weigh more on her mind than Kat. Images of Jordan flickered behind her eyelids. Their last happy night together. The curve of her soft thigh, the tendons lining the sides of her neck, her smile, and how her breasts felt pressed against Kat's chest.

Her mind turned to her fling with AJ. Kat realized she knew nothing about AJ besides what she did on the Vesta mission. She wondered if AJ's good work would amount to nothing when they hit the ground. At this velocity, nothing would be salvageable, except maybe some of their bone fragments. The body could be surprisingly resilient sometimes. Kat opened her eyes and reached for AJ. Her fingertips brushed AJ's bicep. She knew this body. She'd become one with this body once upon a time. In the face of their fiery demise, it seemed foolish to call off their short-lived romance for insubstantial reasons.

AJ turned to face her. Tears were streaking down AJ's face. Kat could still hear Commander Cavanaugh barking out orders. Kat unbuckled herself and grabbed onto her seat so she wouldn't fly backwards from the weight discrepancy between her and the ship at freefall.

A SCENE FROM *DOS LESBOS:* COMING OUT AT WORK—OR NOT!

Terry Baum

(Peg is discovered reading the newspaper.
Gracie enters, kisses Peg, throws herself into a chair.)

Gracie: Hi, hon. How'd it go today?

Peg: I can't understand it. I did everything Ronald Reagan told me to do. I answered every single want ad in the paper, and I'm still unemployed. Maybe I should take up typing.

Gracie: Please don't *speak* to me about typing.

Peg: How was *your* day?

Gracie: Don't ask. I don't want to talk about work. I don't want to think about work. Every day I have to go out on the streets and sell my fingers to the highest bidder. So just don't ask me about work.

Peg: Alright, I won't ask.

Gracie: I had a very traumatic experience at the office today. I was a coward. The coward of Abromowitz, Rodriguez and Chan, attorneys at law... esquire. It was disgusting. Why didn't I say something? Why didn't I *do* something?

Peg: Tell me.

Gracie: Really?

Peg: I'm all ears.

Gracie: You're so cute when you're all ears. (*she kisses Peg.)* So it was about a quarter to eight, before work started. We were all standing around the coffee cart, talking about our weekends. And Nancy Nice says, "I went to the wildest party..."

Peg: (*interrupting*) Nancy Nice? I think I'd kill myself if my last name was "Nice."

Gracie: (*warning*) You're all ears, remember?

Peg: Sorry. So, Nancy Nice...

Gracie: Anyhow, so Nancy Nice goes to this wild party, right? And she sees some dirty movies there, right? "It was awful," she says. "But," she says, "At least it was a man and a woman, if you know what I mean." Everybody *laughed.*

Peg: Except you.

Gracie: Except me. And then she said it again, just in case we all hadn't heard it the first time. "At least it was a man and a woman, *if you know what I mean.*" I was furious. I wanted to say something. I wanted to do something. I thought of fifty things to say. I almost said one of them. But they would have thought I was a jerk – partly because I was a lesbian, but mainly because I got upset when they were having a good time. So I said nothing. (*sarcastically*) "At least it was a man and a woman."

Peg: If you know what I mean.

Gracie: If you know what I mean.

Peg: (*comforting Gracie*) They're idiots. You know that. You shouldn't let them get to you.

Gracie: I just didn't want to be a pill and ruin a good time. I just wanted to be one of the gang.

Peg: Don't be so hard on yourself. It takes a while to figure out what to do in situations like that.

Gracie: By the time I've figured it out, the situation is all over. Nancy Nice insulted me, and she doesn't even know it. Why didn't I say something?

Peg: You know what you need?

Gracie: What?

Peg: You need the Charlene Atlas Course in Word-Lifting!

Gracie: Word-lifting?

Peg: That's right. Through a series of gradual exercises, you train yourself to talk back, to lift those heavy, heavy words that have a tendency to get stuck at the back of your throat when you're offended.

Gracie: Mine seem to stay down somewhere in my diaphragm.

Peg: In your diaphragm? That's serious.

Gracie: Oh no!

Peg: But, not to worry! Charlene Atlas will teach you to bench press those courageous rejoinders, lifting them from deep down in your diaphragm, up to your esophagus, past your vocal chords – and actually say them to someone.

Gracie: No kidding!

Peg: Are you tired of having insults kicked in your face at the office?

Gracie: You bet.

Peg: Are you sick of having innuendos hurled at your head in the street?

Gracie: I sure am.

Peg: Are you fed up with ignorant assholes trampling on your tenderest feelings?

Gracie: You'd better believe it, sister.

Peg: Then Charlene Atlas has the answer for you! Her guaranteed, foolproof course in Word-Lifting!

Gracie: When do I start?

Peg: Right now. First, close your eyes and say to yourself "I am a lesbian."

Gracie: (*closes and then opens her eyes.*) Okay. I did that.

Peg: Now, say it out loud, not to anyone in particular.

Gracie: (*looking around*) I am a lesbian.

Peg: Now, look at me when you say it.

Gracie: (*looking lovingly at Peg*) I am a lesbian.

Peg: Now…Imagine I'm Nancy Nice. (*taunting*) At least it was a man and a woman. At least it was a man and a woman.

Gracie: You have to say, "If you know what I mean." That was the worst part.

Peg: Right, I forgot. (*bears down on Gracie, who backs away.*) At least it was a man and a woman, if you know what I mean. At least it was a man and a woman, if you know what I mean. If you know what I mean, if you know what I mean…

Gracie: (*disconcerting and mumbling*) Nancy Nice, I'm a…

Peg: (*driving her into a corner*) A man and a woman, a man and a woman, if you know what I mean, if you know what I mean!

Gracie: (*pulls herself together and turns the tables*) Nancy Nice, what's wrong with a Woman and a Woman? Do you think it's disgusting, perverted? Do you think that we're all too nice here in this staff room to have ever done IT with a woman? You're wrong, Nancy Nice. You may be nice, but I'm not nice at all. (*caresses "Nancy Nice" while she moans in horror*) I'm a bad girl, a nasty girl. I do it with a woman all the time. Nancy Nice, I AM A LESBIAN! (*"Nancy Nice" collapses*) And I don't like *you* making fun of it, *if* you know what I *mean*!

Peg: (*leaping up*) Congratulations! Here's your certificate of graduation. (*she hands Gracie the funnies from the paper she was reading*)

Gracie: (*thrilled with herself*) I am a lesbian!

Peg: You are now qualified to bring up a host of unpleasant subjects in daily conversation, such as your own homosexuality...

Gracie: (*striking a pose*) I am a lesbian!

Peg: .... The need to raise taxes...

Gracie: (*another attitude now*) I am a lesbian!

Peg: And various other topics that people would really rather not even think about.

Gracie: (*climbs on a chair to tell the world*) My fellow Americans, I am a...LESBIAN!

(*blackout*)

POCKETKNIVES, HOODIES, AND QUILTS: A LESBIAN READER

Cecilia Kiely

> It's a patchwork and the threads aren't always neatly tied. Let's call it a quilt. You can make a quilt out of flannel and denim and plaid and old ripped hooded sweatshirts. And you can drape it on anything—your futon, your cat, the backseat of your Subaru.

> "This is not a quote-unquote real novel," Eileen Myles says about *Cool for You*. "It's *my* kind of novel—pasted together and funky. While writing this book, I thought, It's going to explain more than novels are supposed to; it's just going to do any fucking thing it wants to do, and then I'm going to say it's a novel when I'm done."

I read to fill in my sketchy background in lesbian literature. I thought the first step would be simple—read works by lesbian writers—but hadn't anticipated a fundamental problem: I don't know what a lesbian writer is. I had never even considered that Faulkner might be one. Re-searching the elusive lesbian narrative took over my read-ing: I went through every book in the library with these two highly contested terms as keywords, hopping from

> **Liz Lemon:** I'm on humanity leave.
> **Jack Donaghy:** Good God, what Indigo Girls song is that from?
> **Lemon:** "Syllabus of Us." It's off *Vagabonds, Martyrs and Quilts*.

theorist to critic hoping to get to the source—which as far as I could tell was only a deep well of lone-liness. And not even *The Well of Loneliness* because can that even

> Audre Lorde's *Zami: A New Spelling of My Name*, was published in 1982, the year I was born. She called it "biomythography."

Reading between the lines is not hard to do when you grow up with an eye for the unspoken. Who else but other queers have a classic film canon of movies that don't even acknowledge their existence? *Thelma & Louise. A League of Their Own.* They even turned *Fried Green Tomatoes* into just another hetero narrative, removing the explicit (i.e. acknowledged) lesbian romance before making the book into a movie.

That's the beauty of it. You can make a lesbian movie that also caters to straight women. Just create an unnecessary plot line with an attractive male love interest (e.g. *Bend It Like Beckham*). We can always see what is really going on. Plus, we love yet another chance to calibrate our lesbian specs.

be considered a lesbian narrative if the narrator/author is a self-hating invert?

Though my reading list was formed around the idea of defining a literary tradition, I was ultimately not interested in debating what makes a book lesbian or not lesbian. I wanted to know instead why I write like I do and how it relates to my being queer. From this angle, I was able to see how my writing has been shaped by the kind of reader I am.

I am a lesbian reader. I have always "read into" things and this is not because I am a natural academic, but rather because I grew up trying to find my lesbian story in heterosexual narratives. I adapted, claiming stories as my own even before realizing why or how I was doing it. From the way I read books like *My Ántonia* in high school to the way that I connect with lesbian writers such as Alison Bechdel and Eileen Myles today, my experiences as a lesbian reader have informed my writing.

I write *for* the lesbian reader, but I write to *create* lesbian readers as well. I attempt to re-create my own reading experience for others through the way I write literary collage.

Looking at what it means for me to be a lesbian reader, I also explore how this type of reading can connect individuals and

> I went to see the doctor of philosophy/with a poster of Rasputin and a beard down to his knee/He never did marry, or see a B-grade movie/He graded my performance/He said he could see through me/I spent four years prostrate to the higher mind/I got my paper and I was free.
>
> —Indigo Girls, "Closer to Fine"

form a unique lesbian literary culture. Examining how we must often create our own narratives as both readers and writers, I find ways that lesbians use storytelling to claim space and resist stereotypes. Relating these ideas to my own writing, I look for ways to connect with other lesbians while also engaging the lesbian reader in all of us.

This is my relationship to my reading—an understanding of how my lesbian lens affects the way that I read and write. This is my critical essay—pasted together.

I | The Lesbian Reader
In which we put on our specs and start seeing lesbians everywhere.

Reading like a lesbian can mean uncovering your own story in a heterosexual narrative the same way you discovered your queer identity in a heteronormative world. For me, reading as a lesbian means making meaning of snippets, patching together scraps I take as clues, and going beyond the limits of what is written on the page. Being queer requires a closer reading of social situations, a constant negotiation of identity, so it's no wonder that I grew into a literature student who enjoyed going beneath the surface of texts. I have always approached my reading with the idea that the hidden story is often the more interesting one.

I read with what Gillian Hanscombe calls "lesbian specs" ("Katherine Mansfield's Pear Tree" in *What Lesbians Do in Books*, edited by Elaine Hobby and Chris White. London: The Women's Press, 1991: 111). (She's British.) She writes, "Sometimes being a lesbian reader is rather like being one of the favored few in the cinemas of the 1950's who were given red and green specs so they could see the breathtaking perspectives of the new 3-D movies. Audiences without the specs saw only the usual thing; and sometimes not even all of that. But with the specs, all was revealed." Of course, the usual thing is a heterosexual plot.

Sally Munt, referring to Roland Barthes distinction between "readerly" (lisible) and "writerly" (scriptible), suggests that the "lesbian culture's ability to be so *writerly*" is because "lesbian readers must rewrite texts, heterosexual or lesbian, as they read." Again this tendency reflects the way lesbians exist in the world. Lacking the social scripts that straight people take for granted, queers are often left to write their own.

> Every book is a lesbian book.
> –Dorothy Allison

It makes sense—if you're not given a narrative you either have to create one for yourself or continue to exist in the margins. "Reading into things" is an adaptation, a survival mechanism. The facts are usually not on our side, not playing for our team. Nancy Drew has a boyfriend. So you search for the story between the facts.

> Everyone says that their first lesbian book was Radclyffe Hall's wretched "Well of Loneliness," but that didn't do it for me. . . . If you limit the list to self-defined lesbian books, then we get down to just one: Rita Mae Brown's "Rubyfruit Jungle." But looking for self-defined lesbian books was never how I approached the subject. I always reinterpreted books to give me what I needed. All books were lesbian books — if they were believable about women at all, and particularly if they were true to my own experience.
>
> –Dorothy Allison

For me, this literal marginalization creates a desire to represent personal experiences in my work in order to give still underrepresented stories space on the printed page. But more importantly, my experience as a reader gives me an awareness of, and an appreciation for, what is left unwritten.

According to Nicky Hallet, author of *Lesbian Lives: Identity and Auto/biography in the Twentieth Century,* "Lesbian readers are hungry readers. . . . For a heterosexual woman, the idea that she should seek out evidence that there are others around is nonsensical. Detecting testimony of other lesbian existence is an occupational habit of lesbians. Signs of life are sought in many places. This sounds desperate: it is often celebratory, and most of all it is habit forming."

For many lesbian readers, looking for these signs of life starts early. In childhood I quickly picked up on the ways in which I was different from other girls, but I didn't have a way to make sense of these differences. Knowing the typical girl narrative did not fit, I gravitated towards books about boys—the Hardy Boys over Nancy Drew, even *Little Men*, a little-known sequel, over the classic *Little Women.* I enjoyed *Little Women* much more than I thought I would when I eventually read it, possibly because of a lesbian subtext I picked up on; though any complexity was lost on me, I remember at least finding tomboyish Jo to be more interesting than

> The books we read when we were children shaped our lives; at least they shaped our imaginings, and it is with our imaginings that we live.
>
> —Willa Cather

> Whatever is felt upon the page without being specifically named there—that, one might say, is created. It is the inexplicable presence of the thing not named, of the overtone divined by the ear but not heard by it, the verbal mood, the emotional aura of the fact or the thing or the deed, that gives high quality to the novel or the drama, as well as to poetry itself.
>
> —Willa Cather

most other girls I had read about. Of course, in the end she gets married.

In high school English class, I didn't realize that I was reading *My Ántonia* as a lesbian reader since I didn't even identify as a lesbian. If pressed to articulate why I unexpectedly enjoyed the book, I might have guessed that it had something to do with the way Ántonia was called alternately by her full name and by the nickname Tony. I had always been jealous of girls with androgynous names. But looking back, the main reason the story resonated was because it had been written by a lesbian, though I didn't know it at the time. The novel struck a chord with me because it expressed the same latent dissatisfaction I was beginning to feel with the heterosexual plot, though I couldn't name that either.

As Lillian Faderman notes in her anthology of lesbian writing, *Chloe + Olivia*, a "lesbian sensibility often reveals itself" even in novels like *My Ántonia* that on the surface appear to fit into the heterosexual narrative. She says, "That sensibility is suggested sometimes by an expression of strong feminist values—a jaundiced look at heterosexual institutions such as marriage, a yearning for agency and independence—coupled with a determined flexibility in the conception of gender roles. It is suggested more subtly by the gaze that falls lovingly on the female image and the blurred presentation of the male image" (Faderman: 1994). The beauty of lines like Lena's, "I don't want to marry Nick or any other man,"

> Question: Is Tony jealous that he gets to kiss her or that she gets to kiss him instead of her?
>
> Let's say Jim was a woman instead like Tony and Lena. We would ask:
>
> Is Tony jealous that she gets to kiss her or that she gets to kiss her instead of her?
>
> And we would see the limitations of pronouns are more pronounced when discussing lesbian relationships

is that they work equally well for just a regular old independent badass pioneer woman as they do for a badass lesbian pioneer woman.

In *My Ántonia*. Cather shows Tony become jealous when Jim tells her that Lena lets him kiss her: "'Lena does?' Tony gasped. 'If she's up to any of her nonsense with you, I'll scratch her eyes out!'" (1994). Now if that's not dyke drama, I don't know what is.

More than ten years after graduating high school, I am now so used to seeing through my lesbian specs (I wear them all the time, not just for reading, which sometimes gives me a headache) that often the books on my lesbian list nearly shocked my system. Not that I hadn't read about lesbians before, but for the first time, reading Michelle Tea and Eileen Myles and Alison Bechdel, it wasn't me trying to decode closeted or veiled insinuations. These authors were acknowledging a sort of shared experience. They were meeting me halfway, and I didn't feel like I had to search for the lesbian story—we were on the same page. It's hard to describe this.

In her graphic memoir *Fun Home*, Bechdel describes buying a Swiss Army knife after getting an unsupportive letter from her mother in response to her coming out. "A symbol of self-reliance?" she wonders. "At any rate, it seemed

> We're going to do a song that I wrote for Virginia Woolf. I wrote papers about her in college but I didn't know what I was talking about. And then a few years ago I got a copy—my mom's a librarian so she gives me all these cool books, or loans them to me, I should say. It was a copy of her abridged diaries and I started reading her diaries– [Fan yells "I love you!" She responds "Love you, too." Crowd cheers.] Anyway, she became my friend through the pages and it was a connection through time and human beings can affect each other. It's very profound and how we're each a part of that so this is what this song is about.
>
> –Emily Saliers of the Indigo Girls

like something a lesbian would have" (Bechdel: 2006). In at least three of the other books I read, I picked up on references to pocketknives. But here the author was making explicit the subtext I was creating. We were sharing a lesbian joke.

Many of the queer writers I work with are motivated by the idea of "writing the book that you wish you read in high school." Constantly re-interpreting texts to give you what you need is exhausting, so it's not surprising that many lesbian (and other queer) readers view writing as a way to make it easier for the next generation of queers to find their stories. But this has always been an abstract concept for me. When I read *Fun Home*, I realized that it was the book I wish I could have found in seventh grade, not in grad school when I was almost thirty years old.

> The single story creates stereotypes, and the problem with stereotypes is not that they are untrue, but that they are incomplete. They make one story the only story.
>
> – Chimamanda Adichie

Another author I wish I had discovered in high school, Dorothy Allison, recognizes that her motivations for writing are tied to the importance that books had in her own childhood. She says that

reading books as child was how she "had kept [herself] semi-sane and developed an idea of how to love someone, how to be part of a community and maybe even find happiness." But these lessons didn't come from the books themselves, but rather from the way she learned to approach her reading. Not having access to lesbian stories, Allison turned the ones she did have into lesbian narratives. She says, "I had spent my adolescence reinterpreting the reality of every book, movie and television show I had ever experienced — moving everything into lesbian land." Reading as a lesbian allowed her to create her own ideas of how to live as a lesbian.

For Bechdel, the process of reading is also closely linked to her process of identifying as a lesbian. She writes, "I realized in the campus bookstore, that I was a lesbian." We later see the scene of her self-discovery—in bed. But she is alone with a stack of books on the nightstand—*Lesbian/Woman, Orlando, Rubyfruit Jungle, The Well of Loneliness, Desert of the Heart.*

But her reading doesn't stop there. We see her in bed again, and this time she is not alone. A lover is reading aloud from *James and the Giant Peach*: "The walls were wet and sticky, and peach juice was dripping from the ceiling. James opened his mouth and caught some of it on his tongue." In the picture, they are both naked, except the lover is wearing her glasses to read.

II | Lesbian Culture

In which we explore how the lesbian reader fits into the larger culture.

In the middle of "*L in L*" (as the *The Lesbian in Literature* was called according to the introduction) is a photo spread that looks like a sixth grade yearbook—badly cropped black and white photos of lesbian authors, from a photo of a bust of Sappho to a portrait of Emily Dickinson to contemporary writers captured in candid shots taken in someone's backyard or awkward headshots in front of brick walls. One is of a young Mary Oliver wearing what appears to be a black turtleneck and a denim anorak. She's one of the only poet's names I recognize, but I don't recognize her face at first. She's looking off to the side. I don't think of Mary Oliver as being young or dykey. I'm not sure how this is important, but it feels like it is.

A   This symbol, A, following an entry indicates major Lesbian characters and/or action.

B   This symbol, B, following an entry indicates minor Lesbian characters and/or action.

C   This symbol, C, following an entry indicates latent, repressed Lesbianism or characters who can be so interpreted. This type of behavior is properly termed "variant" behavior.

T   This symbol, T, following an entry indicates that regardless of the quantity of Lesbian action or characters involved in the book, the quality is essentially poor. The "T" is for "trash."

Lesbian literary culture is not as much a collection of specific texts as it is a lens that connects lesbian readers. Reading as a lesbian can be a way of connecting with other lesbians without getting stuck on defining who or what should be a part of a lesbian canon. Since almost no one is born into lesbian culture, and since it is one of few cultures that people are introduced to through members of their own generation, such as friends or sexual partners rather than older family members, transmitting traditions from one generation to the next has always been a challenge. Either you date an older lesbian, which can be problematic when they see their role as "instructor" rather than partner, or you rely on friends your own age to help you patch together your own ideas of what it means to be a lesbian. Either way, much is lost from generation to generation.

In *The Safe Sea of Women*, a collection of lesbian-feminist literary criticism, Bonnie Zimmerman suggests that lesbians of her generation have created a lesbian culture. "We mix together Sappho, amazons, Gertrude Stein, and Natalie Barney . . . . add bar culture from the fifties; season liberally with new left politics and new age consciousness; strain through traditional literary metaphors; and cover over completely with feminism to produce a lesbian culture." Not only is that lesbian culture they've cooked up fairly limited to a white, middle-class perspective as it's "covered over completely" with a feminism that often alienated women of color

> Brave and forthright and insightful—exactly what Alison Bechdel does best.
>
> –Dorothy Allison's blurb for *Fun Home*

and working class women, but Zimmerman also overestimates how effectively this new lesbian culture can be passed down. She says, "Today when a woman comes out as a lesbian, she has an identity and a belief system waiting for her should she choose to embrace it." Yet this is exactly the thing—a cultural identity cannot survive if it is static, "waiting" to be embraced. Quickly the culture becomes outdated, less relevant to the younger generation. (Case in point: I have no idea who Natalie Barney is.)

Forming community around common strategies for discovering identity instead of the false notion that lesbians share a single story allows for a more inclusive culture. This makes more sense—the lesbian specs can be developed and nurtured. It's not about the representation in texts of a lesbian culture or ideal lesbian community, but rather the way that the books themselves are used to connect. For example, in 1981, the third edition of *The Lesbian in Literature* was compiled by Barbara Grier and published by Naiad Press. The first edition had been published in 1967. This book was essentially a bibliography of every book that was written by a lesbian or written by someone who might be a lesbian, or that had lesbian characters or a character that might be a lesbian, or had a character that would have played softball or wore dungarees if they had the chance.

For over fourteen years, the *L in L*, along with their literary publication *The Ladder*, formed a network of lesbian readers across the country. While ostensibly telling lesbians where to look for lesbians in literature, it was just as much showing

A review of *Cool for You* in the *San Francisco Guardian* written by Michelle Tea, no byline just her name in parentheses at the end of the capsule review: "With grace and anger, Myles reveals and accuses; she's a butch dyke Bukowski whose confessions clear a place at the table for her queer, working-class sisters while hurling bottles at the larger culture that continues to kick them to the curb."

lesbian readers that they weren't alone in their interpretations, that they weren't the only ones reading the way they did, gauging the sexuality of characters based on subtle clues in the text. In the foreword to the third edition, Maida Tilchen describes finding novels in a used bookstore, A-B-C-T ratings penciled in. She writes,

Once, in a tiny rural bookstore, I found a book that looked relevant and that had a 'B' written on the cover in delicate handwriting. Checking the bibliography, I found that it certainly was a 'B.' I felt a great affinity to the unknown woman who had also been using the bibliography. And I felt a great sadness, wondering why she had ever let the book slip back onto the bookstore's shelves. Had she died and her estate been dispersed? Had she needed the money so desperately that she sold the book? Or, as I discovered after years of book collecting, had her shelves and closets overflowed so much that she regretfully decided to unload some of the less important books?

Notice the stories she tells herself about this previous reader. She creates an entire narrative— multiple narratives even—from a single penciled

Eileen Myles's blurb for *Valencia:* "Michelle Tea's second book is really brave. If you want to know how dangerous and great and awful it is to be a girl, you'll scarf *Valencia* right up. There's so much colliding and 'sharing.' I mean in the good way—sharing bodies, drugs, stories, and clothes. The street today is full of girls, if you haven't noticed."

"B." Here the facts don't matter. The "B" could have been an initial of the owner or maybe a grade assigned independent of the lesbian rating guide, perhaps by an overzealous writing professor compelled to grade all his books like student papers. It's not the actual story but the story that Tilchen is able to construct for herself from these clues. Here we see inherent *writerliness* of the lesbian reader.

Just like the *L in L* itself, this story is about claiming these signs of life, validating them, saying to yourself, "See, you're not the only one who thinks Amelia Earhart was a little gay." Even though this book was essentially a lesbian canon, or at least a

> Michelle Tea, another queer working-class writer, who also grew up in the poor outskirts of Boston. In *Valencia* she writes, "I had just discovered Eileen Myles." This comes before mentions of Ani DiFranco, and tofu and tahini.

reading list, it wasn't what was being read that connected lesbians, but rather the way in which they were reading these books. So when Tilchen calls the book the "Legendary Lesbian Treasure Map," I disagree. If it is a treasure map, it is one that is less about ultimately finding the treasure than simply finding the map, which tells you you're not the first one to ever wash up on this island.

III | Lesbian Storytelling

In which I read the pocketknife as a lesbian reader and connect a literal carving of space to a figurative one, suggesting the importance of storytelling.

Lesbians are hungry for stories of other lesbians. Mainly because lesbians remain erasable, especially in the male-centered heterosexual narrative that we still see continually played out, in everything from novels to car commercials. So we tend to look for the little clues and let our imaginations run wild. One example of my being a hungry reader is the way I picked up on independent references to pocketknives in at least three of the books—*Fun Home, Zami, Bastard out of Carolina*; it was an object that stuck out to me because of my associations between Swiss Army knives and tomboys. It wasn't enough to simply note this coincidence; I had to make it *mean* something.

> We'll leave the figuring to those we pass on the way out of town.
>
> –Indigo Girls, "Get Out the Map"

On one level, mention of a pocketknife can be seen an easy shorthand to show that the girl is self-reliant. The way that the jackknife can be read in *Bastard* shows why every young lesbian, or at least every independent young girl, needs a pocketknife.

Drawing on greater implications of the object, Allison uses the knife to show the importance of changing your own narrative. What do kids do with pocketknives in books? They become blood brothers (back in the day). Make literal a bond between friends with whom you feel a kinship but don't share blood.

What else do young people do with pocketknives? Carve their names into branches. Carve their lover's name into the trunk. These etchings are a literal way to stake a claim, make space, the way that writing can in a larger sense. Audre Lorde writes that as a child she used the penknife that her father always carried around in his bathrobe pocket to sharpen her pencils.

> It's a biomythography, which is really fiction. It has the elements of biography and history and myth. In other words, it's fiction built from many sources. This is one way of expanding our vision.
>
> –Audre Lorde, on *Zami*

In *Bastard out of Carolina* Allison also shows this imaginative link between the literal carving power of a knife and the figurative power of narration to create space for marginalized identities: the main character, Bone, highly values both jackknives and storytelling. Expressing the need to have something useful, something to give her power usually reserved for boys and men, Bone says, "Some days I would grind my teeth, wishing I had been born a boy. ... I begged my aunts for Earle's and Beau's old denim workshirts so I could wear them just the way they did when they worked on their trucks, with the front tucked in and the tail hanging out." (Allison: 1992). Here Allison is not saying, "Bone is a baby dyke," but by presenting her experience as one where gender is complicated, she conveys something that lesbian readers can identify with, even if they spent their childhoods dressing up in tiaras instead of overalls (or maybe both). Bone is breaking out of the narrative that has been given to her when she was born a girl.

How To Use Your Dyke Multi-tool
1. Carve space for yourself
2. Cut (yourself out of) boxes
3. Question everything, especially things men tell you about lesbians
4. Appreciate double entendre
5. Pry the story out from between the lines
6. [Not sure what this is for]
7. Patch together your history & culture
8. Celebrate your coming out (every time)

WARNING: This tool should NOT be used to poke your eyeballs out in frustration.

Bone continues, "I followed them around and stole things from them they didn't really care about—old tools, pieces of chain, and broken engine parts. I wanted most of all a knife like the ones they all carried—a Buck knife with a brass-sand-stained-wood handle or a jackknife decorated with mother-of-pearl. I found a broken jackknife with a shattered handle that I taped back together around the bent steel tang. I carried that knife all the time until my cousin Grey took pity and gave me a better one" (Allison: 1992). The actual knife is of no value, broken and tossed aside; it is the power that it represents.

Bone figuratively carves space for herself with her storytelling. Similar to the way Allison does in her memoir *Two or Three Things I Know for Sure*, Bone describes how her stories, usually gruesome and full of adventure, captured her younger sisters' and cousins' attention. Bone also makes up a game to play with her female cousins; she called it "mean sisters." When her sister asks what the mean sisters do, Bone responds, "They do everything their brothers do. Only they do it first and fastest and meanest" (Allison: 1992).

When Bone directs her cousins and sister in playing "mean sisters," she's making a place

> I am watching YouTube clips of the Indigo Girls—their network TV debut on Letterman, back in the day and you can tell how old it is because when he announces they have a new album, he holds up a record. That and David Letterman has hair. He goes, "Please welcome . . . Indigo Girls!" and they walk out, and there must be some dykes near the audience mics because someone is just going "wooooooo!" the whole time. Amy is all punked out in a folk rocky way—black t-shirt, about seven medallions around her neck, and jeans ripped down both thighs. Black acoustic guitar and Emily's is a classic acoustic guitar, shiny wood. Her blond hair is all '80's feathered; she's wearing a bright salmon t-shirt tucked into her jeans, short sleeves cuffed. And I start to tear up in the coffee shop. No joke. I feel a debt to these two that I can't explain.
>
> They are twenty-five, younger than I am now. I was seven and there they were like they were my older cousins on network TV carving out a space for me to grow into being gay.

for herself, and other girls like her, by subverting the masculine heroic narrative, disrupting it and reclaiming it. When her uncle laughs at the idea, her cousin Patsy Ann is embarrassed and points at Bone saying, "She told me about it, she told me I could." Bone is giving other women permission to create their own narratives, and her reaction to the put-down is different; she thinks, "I didn't care. I played mean sisters for all I was worth" (Allison: 1992). The unexpected twist at the end— "I" rather than "it"—suggests there's more here than just a child's imaginative game.

Because lesbians are not given a narrative, they have to create their own. Storytelling has a similar power for Lorde as it does for Allison. In *Zami*, Lorde writes about how her older sisters would whisper each other stories at bedtime: "I thought that the very idea of telling stories and not getting whipped for telling untrue was the most marvelous thing I could think of" (Lorde: 1982). She says her sister Helen's stories "were far and away the best, filled with tough little girls who masqueraded in boys' clothing and always foiled the criminals, managing to save the day" (Lorde: 1982). Again these stories involve challenging gender roles and expected scripts. Lorde writes that her mother taught her, "If you can't change reality, change your perceptions of it."

If lesbian readers create their own narratives from small clues and encoded material in the text as they read, it makes sense that lesbian writers also reconfigure material as they write their own personal narratives. Using the facts of her life but also weaving in other elements, Lorde retells her story to allow for her existence as both a black woman and a lesbian. Sewing in myth and legend, Lorde connects her Afro-Caribbean heritage to her lesbian identity, creating a text in which they are not at odds. Zami

> # Jamais real, toujours vrai.
> –Antonin Artaud
>
> (Opening quote of *Cool for You*: "Never real, always true.")

is "a Carriacou name for women who work together as friends and lovers." This name allows her to reconcile two aspects of her identity, two cultures she belongs to, without choosing one over the other. The full title is *Zami: A New Spelling of My Name*. Note that Lorde is not claiming a new name but rather what she sees as a re-spelling of it. She is not rejecting a limiting identity, but rather reconciling different aspects of her self.

This same idea is seen as Lorde writes about the first "re-spelling" of her name:

> I did not like the tail of the Y hanging down below the line in Audrey, and would always forget to put it on, which used to disturb my mother greatly. I used to love the evenness of AUDRELORDE at four years of age, but I remembered to put on the Y because it pleased my mother, and because, as she always insisted to me, that was the way it had to be because that was the way it was. No deviation was allowed from her interpretations of correct (Lorde: 1982).

Re-spelling is a revolutionary act; it allows one to take one's name, one's identity, from what it "should" be to what it can be. This is the liberating narrative she creates for herself. It is not just the facts of her life, a simple autobiography, but a story that fuses many narratives into one, creating a unified identity. We usually don't see these other stories, which is why many lesbian authors tend to find forms that allow them to be more multidimensional. This is not a purely literary choice but one that allows them to exist.

This is why lesbian writers often use personal material in novel (no pun intended) ways. Like other marginalized groups, lesbians must be

> I discovered that my own life was written invisibly, was squashed between the facts, was flying without me like the Twelve Dancing Princesses who shot from their window every night and returned every morning with torn dresses and worn-out slippers.
>
> –Jeanette Winterson, *Sexing the Cherry*

careful to present their stories in ways that resist surface readings. The way that these authors link storytelling with power suggests that for many lesbians subverting the dominant narrative is a personal issue before it is an artistic question.

The importance of this type of storytelling is seen in the way that many of these writers use autobiographical elements. The way that lesbian writers negotiate the line between fiction and nonfiction mitigates the danger of the "single story." The contemporary authors I chose to

> There is fiction in the space between
> lines on the page and memories
> write it down but it doesn't mean you're not just
> telling stories.
>
> Sometimes a lie is the best thing.
>
> –Tracy Chapman, "Telling Stories"

focus on—Allison, Bechdel, Lorde, Myles, Tea, Winterson—all use autobiographical material in their work. By expanding the idea of personal narrative, they are able to convey personal stories in a way that opens up literary possibilities, pushing on the boundaries of genre like lesbian lives push at the limits of the heterosexual narrative. By presenting their stories as fictional autobiography or "biomythography" or as novels that incorporate autobiographical material, these authors forefront the literary without devaluing the political implications of telling their stories. The writers use the political power of storytelling, while avoiding the danger of having their narratives seen as exemplars.

Something that particularly stood out to me was that three of the books I read—Valencia, *Cool for You*, and *Oranges Are Not the Only Fruit*—were all novels where the protagonist shared the author's name. While all three writers play with this author/narrator tension, Winterson gets the most mileage out of it. Like many writers, she distinguishes the "facts" from the "story": "There were the 'facts,' either threadbare or limiting,

> In *Cool for You*, Myles uses family names to explore relationships, including the one between herself and her grandmother: "I wrote my own name on a pad of paper. Eileen backwards is Nellie. If you turn one of the *e*'s into an *l*" (Myles: 2000).
>
> Genre is gender if you add a *d* and switch the last two letters around. But the relationship is even stronger than that. Both come from Latin *gener-* meaning kind or sort, the word "gender" even developing in Middle English from French *genre*. Gender is used to sort people the way genre sorts literature. Whether we encounter more resistance for expanding genre or gender depends only on the investments of the audience.

then there was the story—which allowed all kinds of possibilities. Much later, in my 2000 novel The PowerBook, I wrote: 'I can change the story. I am the story.' The freedom of narrative is infinite." Rather than being limited by narrative, Winterson is freed by it. She takes ownership of her story.

But what I find much more interesting is how she answers the question in a March 13, 2010 article in *The Times*. Winterson writes of *Oranges*, "The main character in the book is called Jeanette—and so am I. The book is about a young girl, working class, gay, raised in a fanatically religious environment. And yes, those are the broad facts of my life. But I wanted to use myself as both a fiction and a fact because that is how I understood my relationship to the world."

Though this is not an idea unique to lesbian writers, I think it is one that has a particular resonance with lesbians. Even today,

> # Eileen Myles is a genius.
> —Dorothy Allison's blurb for *Cool for You*

lesbians and other queers must be able to relate to the world in a way that is both fact and fiction. Closeted lesbians are often said to be "living a lie," a phrase that suggests not simply that they are

> I'm only supposed to tell one story at a time, one story. Every writing course I ever heard of said the same thing. Take one story, follow it through, beginning, middle, end. I don't do that. I never do.
>
> Behind the story I tell is the one I don't.
>
> Behind the story you hear is the one I wish I could make you hear.
>
> Behind my carefully buttoned collar is my nakedness, the struggle to find clean clothes, food, meaning, and money. Behind sex is rage, behind anger is love, behind this moment is silence, years of silence.
>
> –Dorothy Allison

hiding something but that their reality, their life, is false. Many lesbians can pass as heterosexuals in at least some situations, and they find themselves constantly negotiating when and how they should "come out." Though the narrative of "coming out" is often seen as the big coming of age moment, the reality of the situation is that coming out is not a one-time thing.

The split between fact and fiction is a cognitive dissonance that Winterson feels toward her own name:

I felt that 'Jeanette' was as good a disguise as any, partly because I did not relate to my name. I don't mean that I wish I was called Esmerelda, but from the first, my close friends have all called me something else, usually JW, or some variant of their own. Then, about a year ago, I discovered that I have another name, because I wasn't adopted until I was six months old. Naming had a hidden resonance for me; though I did not know it consciously at the time. I was and was not "Jeanette."

The name at once fits and doesn't fit, and it seems like that is a relationship that many lesbians have with the name they claim, whether it is lesbian, gay, dyke, queer, women-oriented woman, etc. All of these show how you relate to the lesbian culture, which communities you identify with, how you have chosen to construct your own identity. Lorde writes in *Zami*, "But that is why to this day I believe that there have always been Black

> The only two Indigo Girls songs I can think of (out of more than 200) that actually say "gay" or "lesbian" are "It's Alright" and "Second Time Around," respectively.

dykes around—in the sense of powerful and women-oriented women—who would rather have died than use that name for themselves. And that includes my momma" (Lorde: 1982). Though names can be a source of identity, they are also divisive. This is another difficulty in constructing a cultural identity as a lesbian—claiming others as part of your history and heritage when they may reject the name you want to claim for them.

I think this speaks to the motivations, conscious and unconscious, of many contemporary lesbian writers. There seemed to be a resistance towards simply replacing the heterosexual narrative with a new lesbian one, especially a resistance to labels. While many of the texts focus on names, they often question their authority or play on their implication.

Winterson both "was and was not 'Jeanette.'" Lorde writes that before her friend Gennie committed suicide, she had told her that she was going to kill herself. Lorde says, "I both did and didn't believe her." The cognitive dissonance of growing up as a lesbian develops into an ability to hold two seemingly contradictory ideas, like "I like girls" and "I'm straight," and speaks to the ultimate necessity of blending the two into a coherent narrative of identity.

The ability to run multiple narratives simultaneously is shown by these authors as they use pronouns to occupy the space of more than one gender. Myles writes, "This little apartment in Boston's North End. Crying in my workshirt in my room. Really not a girl anymore. A boy on her bed in the world" (Myles: 2000). In Valencia, Tea describes a girlfriend: "She was such a boy, Iris, a boy with a crush on her babysitter." Here playing with pronouns is a way these writers use language to exist in a space between the boxes of gender. Pronouns tend to erase the lesbian experience

> I used to hate it when male singers covered female singers songs and vice versa, they changed the pronouns. The Crystals singing, "and then he kissed me" and the Beach Boys changing it to "and then I kissed her" (retaining the masculine subject, of course, in addition to correcting the pronouns). I liked singing along with the Beach Boys. When I heard the Indigo Girls cover the Dire Straits years later and Amy Ray was singing to Juliet—"I'd do the stars with you anytime"—I was in college I finally put it together what I was reacting to when I listened to oldies.

and identity. When everyone is a "she" it becomes too confusing. Yet for all its ambiguity, the English language lacks a gender-neutral pronoun, which affects how attached we are to categorizing people by gender—without a way to convey both humanity and gender-neutrality at the same time (which rules out "it") it becomes more important to assign genders.

But there is possibility in the inherent ambiguity of our language, and Myles finds a freedom in this. For her, freedom from gender comes in the form of a misheard word, or rather an ambiguous name. She writes about her Aunt Anne: "Aunt Dan was like Adrien, Sandy or Lee, a name that means person, not woman or man" (Myles: 2000).

This is what it is about—not that Aunt Dan was a lesbian or a gay uncle or whatever. But that there was a way that one could attempt to escape the gender binary, even if in a subtle and ultimately unsuccessful way. Winterson writes an entire book, *Written on the Body,* with a "genderless" narrator. She is careful to never use pronouns. Some argue that this erases a lesbian identity. Yet reading it, I had no doubt that it was a lesbian narrator. (For one, the narrator was always wearing shorts.) For me, this celebrates the possibility of language, just like Myles and Tea do when they mix pronouns. This is one way that lesbian writers break out of the boxes of traditional narrative.

There's a recent Tide commercial with the mother sitting on a couch, upholstered in the worst combination of preppie and yuppie, wearing a pink cardigan and white skirt. Her young daughter, in a camouflage hoodie and olive cargo shorts, plays with blocks on the floor.

"Well, we tried the whole pink thing. Nope. All she wants to wear is hoodies. Hoodies and cargo shorts. Getting dirty. Then she left some crayons in her pocket and they went through the wash. I thought all her clothes were ruined. Enter Tide [here is where her voice gets slightly hysterical] and Tide Booster. The stains are gone, so . . . it's kinda too bad. [Fake smile] Another car garage, honey? It's beautiful."

These writers also subvert the traditional narrative by signaling to readers in different ways, allowing them to connect with a lesbian audience while at the same time avoiding stereotypical readings from non-lesbian readers. A lesbian reader can create an alternative narrative from only bits and pieces and Myles plays on this. In *Cool for You*, she tells us that her family rented their downstairs apartment to two women, but she gives us just the information that she had at the time, knowing she doesn't have to spell it out. Describing one of the women, she says, she "wore a sweatshirt and jeans like me" (Myles: 2000). And to confirm what you're thinking, Myles writes that her mother "was not very impressed by those ladies but at least they wouldn't have kids." But it's not just that Myles is demonstrating that she doesn't have to say "lesbian;" it's that she's showing us the process of identification, as though she's not quite sure yet but she knows they are alike in some way—she wears "sweatshirts and jeans like me." The lesbian reader is likely to pick up on this association more quickly as it might mimic a similar experience in their own life, or at least the importance of this moment would be on their radar.

Another example of where the narrator's process of identification is highlighted rather than identifying the characters for the reader is the way we meet Bone's Aunt Raylene in *Bastard out of Carolina*. Bone identifies with her aunt, who we learn near the end of the book is in fact a lesbian, but I know that as soon as she is introduced, reading her outsider identity as a lesbian identity. Compared to her sisters, Raylene "was quieter, more private, living alone with her dogs and fishing lines, and seemingly happy that way. She had always lived out past the city limits, and her house was where the older boy cousins tended to go." Bone learns from her cousin Butch that Raylene "had worked for the carnival like a man, cutting off her hair and dressing in overalls. She'd called herself Ray, and with her short, stocky build, big shoulders, and small breasts, I could see how no one questioned her." Bone says, "It was astonishing to imagine running off like that, and I would think about it with wistful longing." Again, it is the process of identification that is emphasized. Bone doesn't identify with her aunt because she is a lesbian (ambiguity intended), but because of her aunt's independence. Like Myles's

> "What Makes a Gay Song?" a Time Entertainment blogger asks. She recognizes that the Indigo Girls are a part of nineties gay culture.
>
> "But is their music gay? Folk music itself is a political form and deeply entrenched in the 1970s lesbian-power movement. The Indigo Girls themselves are two gay ladies. But their songs rarely touch on gay topics. The Indigo Girls are not known for explicit anthems or same-gendered love songs. Yet so much about an Indigo Girls show is very gay."
>
> Is a love song just like everything else—straight until proven otherwise? How is a love song sung by a lesbian not a gay song?

lesbian neighbors, Aunt Raylene is introduced as a character through the young narrator's eyes, mimicking the experience for the reader.

In this way, these lesbian writers are able to introduce incidental lesbian characters without presenting them as one-dimensional stereotypes. It's as if Allison ("Every book is a lesbian book") knows that lesbian readers will pick up on hints in her description of Raylene, and that those same readers will feel validated in the end when she is revealed as a lesbian. Other readers, however, are not reading as closely. Not having a simple label of "lesbian" to put on these independent aunts or sweatshirt-wearing women, these readers are less likely to misread the narrative relevance of the characters.

IV | Why I Write the Way I Do

If you grow up reading between the lines, do you end up trying to write that way, too?

I have always wanted to be subtle—both in the way that young queers test the waters by putting out ambiguous signals and in the way of Djuna Barnes's "I have a narrative but you will be put to it to find it."

> I saw Dorothy Allison speak in a church full of Seattle queers in 2006. And I thought if this is what a lesbian writer can be, I want to be one.

There is safety in the privacy of being a lesbian reader. Writing as a lesbian is met with more resistance; I feel a need to hedge my bets. Maybe this is why I am drawn to collage. I've always delivered jokes deadpan; it's best if the only ones who know you are telling a joke are the ones who get it.

I want to write for the ones who get it. Recognizing how, well, recognized I felt when I read *Fun Home* and *Cool for You*, I want to represent my experience because I believe in the power of sharing stories. Dorothy Allison writes:

Sometimes I wonder if books are as lifesaving for teenagers today as they were for me when I was a girl. But then I go to speak to some group and there are those young people clutching books to their hearts, asking me what I am reading with the same kind of desperate passion I felt whenever I went to a library or bookstore. No doubt it is different these days, but that passion still seems to be there. Books are still where some of us get our notions of how the world is, and how it might be.

But if I actually want to change ideas of how the world might be, I need to reach beyond those who are already imagining those possibilities on their own. Lesbian readers are adept at changing their worlds to make room for themselves—they have to in order to survive. Readers who belong to the dominant group, however, aren't forced to change their perceptions; their reality is constantly reproduced for them and so they never have to reconcile their own stories with the stories they read or hear or see.

> Baby, I know you're not one for bearing witness. And you told me that one wrong move is going to sell you out. And I see that you've kept your word and made it harder than it had to be. I wish I could save you the trouble, baby, give you a little peace of mind.
>
> —Indigo Girls, "Moment of Forgiveness"

My agenda (and, of course, it's gay): I want to turn everyone into a lesbian reader.

While I want to connect with lesbian readers in the way I'm used to connecting to texts, with asides and veiled references and just enough hints that they know it's intentional, I also want to create a reading experience for non-lesbian readers that forces them to be aware of how their own lens affects their reading.

Making my writing more associative than narrative, I like to put the ball in the reader's court. On a basic level, collage writing replicates a lesbian reading experience by putting all readers in the margins, forcing them to make their own connections between the elements. The collage is about creating your own subtext. If lesbian stories often exist between the lines, squashed between the facts, then the collage is a natural form for sharing them.

But the problem with telling a lesbian story in subtext is that only the lesbian readers get it, and those that don't have the experience or context to make the connections are not going to do the work on their own. The trouble with delivering jokes with a straight face is that the ones who don't get the joke don't realize they missed anything. So how do you create a reading experience where members of the dominant group, who aren't used to questioning their role as the universal reader, are forced to wonder what they are missing?

> **Emily**: I took classical guitar lessons for a year when I was twelve years old. And then I stopped taking it. I did it for my dad, really. But I have no regrets 'cause it was really great for my technique and you can always benefit from working your hands in that way. It's very difficult actually; it took a lot of practice and discipline. Um it's . . .
>
> **Amy** [interjecting]: It's not necessary.
>
> **Emily**: It's definitely not necessary.
>
> **Amy**: It helps to do some sort of training, but it's not, it's not necessary.

As I've only recently pinpointed this issue, I don't yet have a solid answer. One attempt I made was a draft of a collage piece, "Billie Jean," that aimed to create a lesbian subtext that would run below the surface story. One thing I did was when I referenced the idea of U-Haul lesbians, I put it in the form of the original joke: What does a lesbian bring to the second date? I put the punch line in a footnote. In workshop, several minutes of discussion were spent wondering about the effect of waiting until a footnote to get the joke. No one acknowledged that the effect would be different for different readers, that some readers might already know the answer before reading the footnote. Would it be more effective if the footnote didn't actually give away the punch line? The ability to play around with the different elements of a text is, for me, an exciting way to test out potential answers to this question.

Another way that I try to create a lesbian reading experience is using juxtaposition to bring in the reader's knowledge of certain experiences, even if they are not their own personal experiences. For example, in "Babe" I ask the reader, "Have you ever played the pronoun game?" This is not to alert the lesbian reader that the way Babe referred to her (possible) girlfriend is related to a queer history of self-policing speech. Rather, I am attempting to signal to a non-queer reader this same connection, creating a context that might not be evoked by the situation otherwise.

But like any other form, the collage essay comes with a set of expectations of what it should be. For example, collagists often use juxtapositions to create new connections between ideas, say, placing an apple next to an orange. The difficulty with this, though, is that depending on your viewpoint, an apple and an orange can either be distinct as they are in our clichéd phrase[1], creating a dynamic tension when placed side by side. Or you could see them as two fruits, similar in almost every respect. (Maybe you should juxtapose the fruit with heteronormativity.[2]) Instead of focusing on the differentials between the passages or images I place together, I use juxtapositions to allow the reader to see the connections, even if they are ones that have been made before. My intent is not to make novel connections but to offer the reader the materials and lenses of a lesbian. By juxtaposing my own stories with the biographies of others, I am attempting to disrupt the way we have been trained to read.

Is that a valid use of the collage form? As I can imagine Eileen Myles might say, I don't fucking care.

---

1 Comparing apples to oranges. Did you think I was going to say something gay instead? Like "oranges are not the only fruit"?

2 J/k.

MISFIRE

Yvonne Zipter

What's in here is mine, she said,
tapping the husk of her head,
a miser guarding her ruby
and emerald thoughts.
                                    That night in January
when my car battery froze
and I spent the night
like a plank on her bed,
her, curling away,
a mimosa frond.
She bought jumper cables
for my Valentine's gift.

I didn't know who'd made her shell
but I thought I could crack it.
A good crack would have aroused
her interest me.
                                    Crossed wires,
crossed desires, a room
with an oceanic bed.
All night, the radiator hiss
and a room desolate
as a candle unlit.

FOR MY SWEETHEART
AT THE END OF AN ORDINARY WEEK

Yvonne Zipter

No one speaks ill
of the arm and sleeve

for how handily they couple.
You and I were inclined

one toward the other
as surely as nonparallel lines.

"Codependables," you dubbed us.
A splash of kismet, then, the cocktail

we've lately come to treasure:
the sidecar—the nonliquid variety of which

demonstrates two bodies,
when joined together,

more stable than either
on their own.

APRICOT: A LOVE POEM

Yvonne Zipter

How it lets me enter without reserve,
thumb meeting thumb at the crack
that arches below its stem, and then:
a parting of the flesh.

How it unfolds like butterfly wings
or like a book in miniature,
gives up its hard brown heart
as if it was never meant to be kept.

How it measures the tongue
against its own firmness,
says sweet but hints at tart
like any seductress who knows her part.

Prunus armeniaca. Armenian plum.
Ancient Persians mused it the egg of the sun.
The Romans thought it precocious,
an early-ripening peach.

Neither plum nor egg nor peach—
it is its own fruit, the dawn
of temptation, a blushing little butt
surrendering to my teeth.

THE BLUE NOTEBOOK

Staci Schoenfeld

April 12-15, 1983

Research

Seventh grade and once a week the bus for gifted
students took us from junior high to junior college.

Seventh grade and I: ran away from home, lost
two flutes and a jacket, was nicknamed Spacy Staci.

At the library at Miami Dade Community College
I picked up a thick book about prescription drugs.

Seventh grade and amber-bottled pills stolen
from my mother's medicine cabinet. Twenty odd

RORER 714 tablets, white and scored down
the middle—Quaaludes, the guide assured me.

The red ones I couldn't find in page after page
of colored photos of pill. Those, I called *Insurance*.

The Attempt

Red pill.
White pill.
Orange juice.
White pill.
Handful of white.

Handful of red.
Chalk taste.
Choke.
Orange juice.
Urge to puke.
You have to be quiet for this to work.
Pills gone.
Lights out.

The Blue Notebook

I can't explain why I hid the folder in my closet like stolen goods, like the makeup I stole from drug stores or the colored paper clips I ripped off from the campus bookstore and wore as earrings, can't explain why I pressed the reasons for killing myself between pages of loose-leaf like flowers, like mementos of a trip, like ticket stubs from a movie. In the emergency room that morning, a curtain separating us from the doctors and nurses, I tell my father the notebook's shoved under a shoe box on the shelf above the bin he built for my toys. When I get home it's gone.

The Plum

Here's what I remember:
just home from the hospital
the deep sigh of my body
burrowing into the sofa.

Holding the plum
my mother handed me
still wet from the sink.

Watching mom and dad fight.
Their mouths moving.
That first bite. The taste.
So unexpected.

At J's 13ᵗʰ Birthday Party

I smuggle in a secret bigger than a birthday gift
covered in blue cardstock and tied with rope

thick as a wrist. Watch as the presents
are unwrapped. Listen as all the girls,

giddy and high on cake and ice cream, tease
each other about who has a crush on who.

Lift my mouth into a smile that says,
Yes, I'm having fun. See. Like a normal girl.

Just like you.
After Stopping to Pick Up J's Birthday Present, My Father and I
Take a Walk at Greynolds Park

We were blanketed in sweat. Walked past the mangroves and
live oaks covered with Spanish moss, the canopy full of air plants
cupping their ears to listen to our words or the call of bird song. I
can't remember what you said. Maybe you asked me why I tried
and maybe I told you some story explaining it away. Maybe I
stayed silent as the gumbo-limbo, with its peeling, sunburnt skin,
a strangler fig closing tighter and tighter around its trunk.

THE SEA CUCUMBER

Staci Schoenfeld

after Elizabeth Bishop

Each year is the same—rows of boys
and rows of girls line both sides
of the hall. Hushed walk to the waiting
bus. Dark green seats stuck to skin.

It's November. Insects scream loud
as car horns. No respite from Miami's
heat. Teachers count students *one-two-three,*
sit, then talk to parents—chaperones

who would rather be anywhere else.
The aquarium isn't far, but the drive
seems long. Kim and Jen make friendship
bracelets and a fight almost breaks out

between two of the boys—Jimmy's kicking
the back of Travis' seat. Each time the driver
hits a pothole, everyone's heads
come close to hitting the roof of the bus.

We're thirteen bottles of beer from the end
of the song, when we lurch to a stop
in front of the Seaquarium. The noise level
rises as excited yells are carried forward

in a tidal wave of sound before we get off
the bus and back in lines. Let loose
upon the grounds, we ignore commands
of *walk, don't run,* fling ourselves into the park.

Our group meanders past the dolphin enclosure,
the stingray exhibit, and the crocodiles
to Discovery Bay, where we learn about sea turtles,
tropical birds, and the other creatures

that inhabit Florida's mangrove forests.
The guide shows off starfish and sea urchins,
calls them echinoderms, which means "spiny skin."
Then she picks up what looks like wet dog poop.

Cries of *gross* ring through our group,
but we step closer as she explains
sea cucumbers can expel their own guts
for protection, then grow them back,

turn inside out, tangle or confuse their prey
with sticky filaments. The rest of the trip
nothing else measures up, and on the ride home
no one mentions the sea cucumber for fear

of not seeming cool. Those of us who liked
them best now share a secret language
all our own. One of shy excitement. A lexicon
of knowing how and what to let go to survive.

THE LATE HOUR

Avery Irons

Kneeling down, Joyce adds an eighth felt pad to the leg of one of her wooden tables. With a shake, she tests the table and is satisfied. It's stable, for now. She pulls herself to her feet and considers testing the others; each of the seven tables in her diner wobbles in its own way. She has her pride and in an ideal world would replace them all, but every day she watches her customers drag the tables to meet their rounded bellies; and rest their over-sized purses, overflowing grocery bags and ample body weight on the table corners. The old men attack them, pounding and slapping them when they laugh, and when they cuss. Even with half of Bedford-Stuyvesant gossiping around her, Joyce can hear the table legs grinding down and sifting away, like her money scraping to dust on her floor.

Her back aches and she decides to call it a day. She'll offer one of the neighbor children a few dollars to check and pad the rest of the legs tomorrow. She ticks through her mental list of nightly chores. All tables and the burgundy formica counter disinfected. White linoleum floor swept and mopped. Storefront window cleaned of fingerprints and splatters. Joyce groans as she realizes she's forgotten to wipe down the chairs. Every day some child (or adult) has dripped ketchup onto a seat, or spilled their soda. With a towel and bucket of hot water, she bathes the first chair. Joyce can only guess that in the thirty years her family has owned the diner, she's done this task at least a thousand times. For the first twenty-seven years she hated it. It's repetitiveness. It's necessity. But in the last three years she has found calm in it. Intently focused on her work—scrubbing the seat, cleaning between the spindles, scouring the bottoms for bubble gum, her mind clears itself of her sadness in the way that it won't as she plods through each day or twists in bed each night. She barely registers the taps on the windows behind her.

When the taps do pierce the calm, Joyce already knows it's Tenny. Only after wringing her dishcloth free of every drop of water, does she turn around. The girl is pressed against the window, looking as shy as a child on an errand. Despite misgivings about her ability to handle time with Tenny tonight, Joyce points the girl to the entrance. As a Joyce-required courtesy, when Tenny steps through the diner's door way, her over-sized jeans are up on her waist and her navy Yankees cap is in hand revealing fuzzy cornrows long overdue for a wash and re-braiding. Tenny's fidgety at first and won't look Joyce directly in the face. It's only when the girl flashes an apologetic smile and stares toward the back bathroom, that Joyce sees the black eye and busted lip. Joyce glances away, not sure what she should say about these injuries, or if it's her place to say anything at all. Conflicted into silence, Joyce leads Tenny behind the counter and holds open a saloon door to the kitchen.

Saul, Joyce's cook, is finishing the last of the pots and pans. He's short but solid for his sixty years. Only the gray edges of his almost bald head betray any real sign of age. He has cooked in trousers and church shoes every day for almost thirty years. His dress shirt always hangs on a hook at the kitchen's edge, leaving only his white undershirt to protect his brown, still muscular arms from popping grease and steam. The Dapper Chef, as Joyce's regulars call him, glances up from his work and scowls at Tenny. His nose twists up. Joyce clears her throat to back him off. The girl doesn't smell. That's the whole point of Joyce letting her use the bathroom when she drops in. For her part, Tenny says "good evening, sir" and scurries into the bathroom. The lock slides as soon as the door shuts behind her.

"Put a burger on, Saul. No cheese. And plenty of fries."

"Kitchen's closed." He bends back to his scrubbing.

Why does the man always have to be so difficult? Joyce inhales to gather back her earlier calm. "The kitchen is open until I say it's closed."

"I'm not cooking for that," he says, nodding his head toward the bathroom. "Your mama and daddy didn't let in riff-raff and abominations from the street. It ain't safe or smart."

"Do I have to do it myself?"

He holds out for a few more seconds before marching his dress shoes over to the freezer for a ground beef patty.

As Joyce starts the coffee machine to churning, her eyes rest on photos of her son Jonathan behind the cash register. The three-by-fives, polaroids and school pictures checkerboard his too-short life. She favors the school pictures. Especially the ones taken when she'd still brushed his hair every morning, insuring a ruler straight part on one side. She remembers taping the photos to the wall, her little boy, the reason for her years of toil over pots of collard greens, roasted chicken, and every kind of pie imaginable. If she had it to do all over again, she'd close the restaurant in a snap and rush them away to some country town where he could've grown up nice and slow. She inspects the last picture she taped, taken a few weeks before his death. Now when she looks at this picture, she can only see all the things she'd wanted to ignore. The sag of his jeans. What the color of his t-shirt really meant. The bulge in his pockets: the beads she refused to let him wear in her presence. "My God," she whispers, "forgive me."

Tenny exits the bathroom and saloon doors refreshed and more relaxed, and Joyce abandons Jonathan's photos. Her back isn't strong enough to carry Jonathan and Tenny at the same time. To keep from having to stand around awkwardly while Saul cooks her food, Tenny has taken to reading the diner wall. Joyce's Place doubles as an accidental storefront museum. The walls are Brooklyn's most thorough and honest record book. At least twenty years of history is taped, tacked and nailed over the faded goldenrod paint that peeks out in little spots. When Joyce took over the restaurant from her mother ten years prior, she was determined to weed through it all and only keep what she deemed important. After weeks of reading the walls, inch-by-inch, she'd learned a good deal about the Civil Rights highs and lows, Vietnam, four presidential elections including a whole two-square feet section for Shirley Chisolm and Jessie Jackson. She didn't take much down and has only added articles about David Paterson and Barack Obama.

When the food is ready, Joyce lays it out on a two-seater by the window. She can always gauge Tenny's hunger by the girl's condiment usage. Tonight Tenny doesn't bother with the ketchup bottle or salt shaker. Joyce never knows if and when Tenny will visit. Sometimes, she drops in once a week. Every once in a while weeks pass between their visits. When the time grows long, Joyce fears the worst. The inevitable. She's seen the pictures taped up on laundromat windows. Telephone poles. Grocery store message boards. Photos of smiling girls. Always brown. Always lost. Too often gone. Who would post the pictures of Tenny? Joyce tries not to wonder. Since she first found Tenny huddled and sleeping in the diner's doorway, Joyce has tried to understand the mysterious ways at work in their lives. She has never known whether Tenny knew it was Joyce's diner that she slept in front of. Either way, Joyce understands why the girl is drawn to her, to this place. It is the same reason Joyce can't bring herself to sell it. It is both of their crossroads.

When Tenny's finished with her food, she wraps her small fingers around the coffee cup as if she's cold even though the autumn night has held its heat. For payment, she gives Joyce a timid smile and her eyes give away her softness—they are a striking hazel amplified by her baby soft brown skin and sobered by the black ring around one.

"What happened?" Joyce gestures to her own eye and lip.

Tenny gazes off into the night. "I fell asleep on the train the other night. Some crazy guy figured out I was a girl and thought he could rob me."

"Train's no place to sleep. I thought you were staying at that shelter for . . . ?" Joyce trails off. She doesn't know how to finish the sentence. How to say the words right. When Tenny first told her she went to Sylvia's Place every night, Joyce had thought she'd meant a friend or relative. It had taken her a few conversations to put it all together. It hadn't ever occurred to her that there were so many kids like Tenny on the street, enough to warrant a shelter.

"Most of the time."

"What about your granny's?"

Tenny shakes her head. "I walked past there the other day. She saw me and went inside. It's okay. Same old, same old."

Joyce stands to refill the girl's coffee cup and twists her slightly rounded frame to ease the tension rooting in her back. Joyce has never been successful at talking the young into staying young. There's too much in the streets and world making them want to grow up fast. It was a lesson she hadn't heeded when she was young. At Tenny's age she was on her way to teenage motherhood—an experience it would take every bit of her strength to survive. "I know you don't want to hear this." Joyce sits their fresh mugs on the table. "But maybe you just gotta go back and do what she says so you can finish your last year of school and get on your feet."

Tenny savors a sip of heat. "It's not about doing what she says. I don't disrespect her house. It's just about who I am and I can't change that."

"You can tone it down, a bit." Joyce's eyes drop to Tenny's baggy t-shirt and slide over to her cap.

Tenny laughs. "Miss Joyce can you imagine me in one of my granny's holy-roller skirts."

Joyce pictures Tenny in an ankle length skirt and head full of curls. The image is ridiculous and she responds with understanding's wry smile.

"I'll be okay. Something will give soon." Tenny's eyes drop back down to her coffee cup. "I'm still on the waiting list for that transitional program."

"Something always gives." Joyce's eyes travel across the room to Jonathan's pictures. Against her will, Joyce traces back their braided troubles. She had stood at the diner's front door trying to cajole Jonathan to leave his trouble-maker friends outside and bus tables for her. He was sixteen and testing his manhood against her motherhood. It was mostly banter. He always did what she asked, eventually. But he'd played too hard that day. Too long. Joyce's mind was unforgivably slow and her arms sluggish with shock. She had registered the creeping car. She barely heard the shots before her only child was spun around, gone before he reached her arms. The tires' squeal stole her eyes from his. Everyone in the car had ducked down except for one. A bandana covered the lower half of his face. His forehead was a soft brown hanging over crumpled hazel eyes.

Joyce thought she'd never see those eyes again. And then the police said they'd made arrests. Surprisingly, the hardest part of the trials was sharing courtrooms with the boys' families. In the end everyone lost a son. And Tenny had lost a brother. Joyce remembers the relief when the judge had sent him upstate, and she remembers how Tenny had cried out—a little girl's sharp whimper. Like her lifeline had been cut. Like the way Joyce had cried when she'd finally been left alone after Jonthan's services ended and her last relatives and friends departed. Leaving her to an aloneness she'd never knew could hurt so much. That cry keeps her from turning Tenny away. This is what Joyce told herself, three months ago, when she came back late one night, afraid she'd left the big lock off the back door and found the girl huddled up and sleeping in the doorway of her restaurant. Once roused, the scared and embarrassed almost-child, had asked to use the bathroom. Against her better judgment, Joyce had let her in, keeping her hand in her jacket, gripped on her mace. She'd given the girl a couple of slices of cake and then locked them both out again. It wasn't until a few nights later, when the girl came fifteen minutes before closing that Joyce really noticed her eyes. Her heart nearly gave out.

Saul rumbles through the saloon doors like a brewing storm. He has donned his dress shirt and his fedora is level and firm on his head. "Time to close up." He says this to Joyce, but his eyes rest on Tenny.

Despite her resolve not to, Joyce flinches. "I got it, Saul."

Saul groans at her like she's a disobedient child. "You don't know these street kids, Joyce. She comes in here learning the routine, watching where you put stuff. How you lock the door. Which part of your purse you keep the keys in. She and her hoodlum friends run out of people to stick-up and there ain't nothing to keep them from coming here."

Tenny trembles. Her chair scrapes as she stands in a rush. "I wouldn't take nothing from you, Miss Joyce. Ever. But I won't bother you anymore. I don't believe in staying where I'm not welcome"

"Sit down, Tendra." Joyce's voice is a growl. Her eyes lock onto Saul. His breaths are loud and hot. He removes his hat and grips it like it's a handle for his anger. For the first time, it occurs to Joyce to wonder why this man is so angry. What's it too him? He's not angry for her. She's never told him the tie between Tenny and herself.

Tenny's eyes bounce back and forth between the two adults in front of her and she lowers back into her chair.

"This is my place, Saul. I'll run it how I see fit. And let in who I see fit. If you got problems with that you can walk on out the door and not look back."

"I'm protecting what yo Daddy built, Joyce." Saul straightens his hat and scowls at Tenny one more time and says, "The Devil is a liar," before marching across the linoleum floor and letting the door slam behind him.

"Wow," gasps a wide-eyed Tenny. The single word is so completely on point that Joyce can't help but laugh. The laughter is so hard, so good and hurts her belly so much that tears leak out of her eyes. She pounds on her own table, which makes her laughter erupt beyond her control. She manages to repeat Saul's last words followed by a "sho nuff."

Tenny smiles kindly, but with a tinge of fright in her eyes.

"I'm okay." Joyce says, her arms holding her stomach. "It's been a long time since I laughed like that." They let the laughter settle around them. Joyce feels warm in a way she hasn't felt in years. She watches Tenny stare at the street.

"Where are you going tonight, Tenny?"

"Downtown to catch a bus."

And Joyce understands. She's going to visit her brother. This understanding punches, but she holds it together.

"How's your brother?" Joyce has never asked this question. The words hurt as they ease out, but there's something empowering about having said them.

"He's sorry." Tenny's eyes have crumpled into the eyes she'd seen years ago out of a car's rear window.

Joyce nods. "We all are, I imagine. Just for our own reasons."

ORANGE & CLEMENTINE

Rebekka Hochrath

I would peel clementines
with juice hands and distribute
each slice with a smile.
I would share my pain
like pieces of ripe oranges
bleeding bittersweet onto skin.
I would take your seeping
reality into my sun dreams
and the tangerines I share
grow thunder. I shake the
groves spawned, the whispered
worlds and promise to stay. You
—broken twigs and sealed wings—
collect my burnt roots.

HER

Rebekka Hochrath

Her honeycombed hair, the cornelian flair of color and pumpkin twines, of a gilded sun in an azure sky, bronzed and glazed with fire, alight with flames and sweet, so sweet, as sweet as heavy peaches on bowing branches. Bees in sun rays, reflections in pools of water, of humming and sizzling, the sizzling of heat on dry grass. Heaps of summer on her bare breasts, her fingertips in motion, burning above the rim of the sand. Then, a twinkling star at the far end of her universe, of how far she could see, farther and farther down into her future. The future in droplets of dew on her lips, of rosy cheeks in her hands, dancing to leaves that settled on wet ground. The smell, the eternal smell of sun lotion in her heart that overflowed. Overflowed with the feeling of fingertips brushing against her pants, the line above her hips between skin and fabric, silken and soft. Tentatively. Slowly. Achingly. Some things, she said, some things I have to remember, she said to herself.

LINDA'S FLOWERS

Genevieve Rheams

Casey was thinking about buying Valley roses but she'd have to put her cigarette out first. Standing across the street, she watched the florist with the yellow apron spray something onto the ferns that hung on either side of the flower shop entrance. She thought that she looked like the kind of lady who wouldn't sell her anything if she walked up to her with a cigarette in her mouth. The florist wore her gray hair in a bun and she had skinny, tanned arms with spots. Maybe she'd smoked when she was younger, before they knew that smoking and sunshine were bad for you, and Casey imagined her back then, having a cigarette on the beach with long, unspeckled arms. Seeing Casey pale and smoking might have reminded her of everything she was no longer allowed.

Casey never used to think like that. It had begun last Tuesday when she and Valley saw the painting that meant nothing. The painting had no form, only purples, blues, and greens that swirled together and came out at her, not loudly, but quietly as she looked at it, like waking up. It'd had the same green as the ferns.

Casey looked at her hands, the empty one and the smoking one, and imagined spraying plants. She'd be afraid she would kill them and she didn't know why, just like how she was afraid that the florist would cough at the sight of her, as if it was Casey that was toxic. It wasn't the cigarette, she thought – it was her, reeking of herself. Bad skin from old acne, unwashed jeans, and only indecipherable glances from Valley. How could Valley love her back, even if she gave her a plant?

And, yes, she realized then that a fern would be better than roses. When they met in first grade, Valley was into dinosaurs. She would show Casey pictures of bones and plant fossils. Were there roses at the time of the dinosaurs? She didn't think so. She imagined a place she'd seen in cartoons with ferns, impossibly tall trees, creatures with dry, saggy skin like the flower shop lady's, and smoke in the sky. But she didn't know if that's what it was really like, she'd never studied time like that. Since last Tuesday, she'd only studied Valley and the painting.

That day Casey had been walking through the museum with her like she'd asked her to. She didn't like art museums because she didn't understand anything she looked at and it made her feel dumb. But she always went if Valley asked her to.

Valley stopped at one point when they were walking and frowned at the wall.

"Are we going to go soon?" Casey asked, scratching the back of her head. She was standing two feet away from her, and two minutes away from falling in love.

"In a minute," she said. "I want to know this one."

Valley always talked like that, as if looking at a painting was like getting to know a person. She wasn't an artist, but was the kind of person who wanted to know everything.

"I need a smoke," Casey whined.

Valley smacked Casey's stomach with the back of her hand. "Stop smoking."

"You can't beat it out of me."

"Come on, look at this," she said. "Help me figure this one out. I'm just not getting anything from it."

Casey sighed loudly because she wanted her to know that she was frustrated. And then she looked at the painting.

It was just colors at first. She thought smugly about how she could have painted it in kindergarten. But then she saw a shape in there – a curve, and then something round like the shape of an eye but it wasn't an eye. It was like the hint of a face of someone she knew, but she couldn't remember who it was.

And she needed to know. She'd been through twelve years of grade school and six years of college and had never really wanted to know any of what she'd learned, but she wanted to know this, this person she'd forgotten, who was lost somewhere in the purple, blue, and green. She kept looking, hoping it would come to her, but instead the painting began to brighten and glow. It was warm, and it felt good.

The goodness made her suddenly aware of her stained T-shirt, her hands that stunk like cigarettes, and the dark bangs that hung in her eyes. Had she combed her hair that day? It was as if the good feeling had caught her sleeping on the couch in the middle of the day, and she was unprepared for company. How long had she been sleeping?

"What am I doing?" she asked out loud.

Valley glanced at her. "We can move on if you want."

Casey looked at her. She had always noticed her long, red hair and green eyes. And since they were fourteen, she couldn't *not* notice the curves of her waist, hips, and breasts. But she'd never really noticed *her*, and she was so often standing right there next to her – this woman who in the first grade had introduced herself to Casey as Valley because her real name (Valerie) wasn't big enough. She couldn't explain it further than that at the time, but she was into dinosaurs back then and she said that her mother was just happy that she hadn't decided to call herself Triceratops. In the twenty-eight years that they'd been friends she had never met another person like her. Valley had been with so many other women. Had she ever noticed Casey the way that she was noticing Valley now?

Was there anything to notice? She was thirty-four, unemployed, living on her mom's couch, and interested in nothing. She'd had lots of bartending and dishwashing jobs in her 20's, and had even been good looking at some point, but those parts of her, the parts of her that added color to the world had fallen asleep. Valley kept telling her how smart she was and how much she thought she could do, but she wasn't sure that she was anything more than a cloud of smoke covered in bad skin.

"Come on," Valley had said to her, shoving her hands in her jeans jacket pockets. "It doesn't mean anything. You want a cigarette?"

Casey looked back at the painting, unable to speak. Valley didn't wait for an answer but walked towards the exit and, after a moment, she followed.

Casey had gone back to the museum every day since then to look at the painting that had meant nothing to Valley. It was on her way back from it that day that she'd noticed the flower shop and thought of roses.

Now she was sure that she was right, roses were wrong for this woman who'd chosen the name Valley because Valerie wasn't big enough. She felt that Valley needed something ancient, something beautiful that was from a history she didn't remember but that Valley knew.

She decided to cross the street and find out how much the ferns were. She had about seventy-five dollars left in her checking account to blow. She was going to have to get a job again soon.

"Jesus," she thought. "What does that mean about me?"

Because since last Tuesday all she did was think about what things meant.

As she approached, the florist smiled and asked if she could help her. Her voice was gravelly but in a soothing way.

"How much is that?" Casey asked, pointing to the dripping fern.

"This is..." the lady pulled a white tag from the hanging pot. "$6.99."

"How old is it?"

"I got it in two days ago."

"No, I mean, when is it from? Was it around, like, in dinosaur times?"

She looked at Casey funny. "Well, I don't know. Maybe not this species but something like it."

"Something like it is good," she said, suddenly afraid that the lady might think she was crazy. She wondered if that were true. "I'll take it."

She smiled at Casey. Casey could tell it was a real smile and not just one that she gave to people who bought things from her.

The smile gave her the confidence to follow the florist inside, where she was stunned and shamed by the beauty of the store. The wall was lined with gray wooden shelves of flowerless plants and orchids, and in the center of the room were two rows of potted rose bushes, lilies, daisies, and other colorful, soft things that Casey couldn't identify. There was a cooler along the wall, and she could see the arrangements inside through the wet, cold glass. It was like being in a cabin with the garden on the inside. The sign on the front of the checkout counter said, "Linda's Flowers."

"Are you Linda?" she asked, pulling her wallet out of her back pocket.

Linda nodded and set the fern on the counter. She began punching numbers into a cash register that was the color of old paper.

"I'm Casey," she said, handing over her check card, and thinking about how that was the first time in her life she'd ever voluntarily told her name to a stranger.

Linda swiped the card and said, "Is this for you?"

"No, it's for my friend. I think she'll like it. I mean, I hope she does," Casey said, brushing her bangs out of her eyes.

Linda frowned at the credit card machine. "It didn't go through, honey."

"It what?"

"Let me try it again. Sometimes it takes more than once."

"It should," she said, thinking about it, remembering the number "seventy-five" the last time she checked her account.

How long ago had that been? She didn't think she'd spent anything since then. Had it been seventy-five cents and she'd looked at it wrong? It couldn't have been.

But after trying the card a second time, Linda shook her head, handed it back to Casey, and apologized.

"It's ok," she said, feeling her face get hot because, really, it wasn't ok. She shoved it all into her back pocket.

Casey turned to leave and Linda said, "Are you all right?"

Casey stopped. "Um, yeah. I just need a job, I guess. Can I ask you a question?"

"Sure."

"Have you ever been in love?"

Linda laughed and when Casey didn't laugh back she said, "Yes."

"How'd that go?"

"Went fine. We were together for 36 years. He died just two years ago."

"I'm sorry."

She shrugged. "It's ok. It was bound to happen to one of us."

Casey smiled sideways at her.

"I think if you want things to go well with your friend you should get that job."

"Probably. Well, thanks."

She turned to leave again.

"Casey," said Linda.

She walked out from behind the counter, to the center of the room, and pulled a pair of scissors from her apron pocket. She cut a red rose from its bush, and held it out to her.

Casey took the flower. She held it lightly to avoid the thorns, so that it tilted in her hand. Linda gave her a grin that ached like the truth of the painting, like the truth of Valley.

When she got home she dropped the flower in a mason jar, set it on the coffee table, and sat back on the couch to stare at it. After a while she dug out a piece of paper and began to draw it, trying to get the lines and the curves right. As she drew her mind wasn't filled with the image of the rose, but of purple, blue, and green bursting like the sunlight that had shocked her eyes when she'd walked out of the flower shop. When she finished the drawing she saw there in the folds of the petals, the face.

PERSÉ

Suzanne Gardinier

I still can't remember when / or how I lost my way
Neil Young, "Cortez the Killer"

I have come upon it, I have come upon blessing,
People, my relatives, I have come upon blessing,
People, my relatives, blessed.
Navajo Blessingway

1

At the edge of the cove near where my mother's / brothers laughed
    & threw nets
The *guanábana* in the sand where they fell / Three palms talking
    in the wind
When I heard them I was dreaming my aunts / laughing when
    Mama say Gather enough
To make a pile like this & her sisters say Dee / Those girls gonna be
    out there all night

& before we left they told us / what to say & which way to turn
& how to listen for what the day / whispered in the night
& when to go & when to stay back The sky / watching the fisher
    birds & the fisher birds watching
Our village as old as the first palm's seed / & new as one wave's spray

& some dead forgetful places When someone / fell out of the
    meshes & lost their balance
The places the soldiers found Embers / they breathed on until you
    could almost not hear
The thickets stammering through burns The stained reefs / The
    choked springs coughing all night

In the places where there had been messages Where we / were
    messages Before the captain came

A new world A flock made a scatter of bones / A nest made a pit
    grave next to a spring
They had to drink too Didn't anyone teach them / what comes up
    from under the ground
Not the gold they preferred to freedom / Not the world they made
    called Hell
Looking down into their own reflection / as the earth called their
    old lost names

That their children would be filling our baskets / with our cut hands
    generations hence
On the banks of the Congo the Solo the Sola / the Mekong the
    Mississippi
That the earth they tried to make kneel as they breathed / on the
    embers of our division
Would burn & their breath become part of the burning / That a
    theft leaves a gap That what's buried grows

Sometimes in the dark of the *cimarrón* caves / I could see the
    design of their plans for us
A net stretched across two trees nailed together / Like the place
    where they tied my aunt's youngest girl
The soldiers fidgeting in a line while they waited / Later one drew
    her With snakes for her hair
But it was fire After they cut her / & put her face where a baby
    would be

This was the place they kept promising us / If I tell you does it make
    it come nearer
Or keep a witness who also remembers / how she laughed with
    guanábana smeared on her cheeks

How we opened & shared one when we were thirsty / The seeds at
    the tideline gone by morning
Scratching our backs on the *cocoteros* / The *cocoteros* thumping
    the beach with food

Scatter them he said Meaning the people / His gesture like flicking
    mosquitos away
In front of the guarded pits for their hoardings / Little prisons for
    gold & food
If we'd had a map of their hell If we'd learned / to breathe there
    long enough to recover
The time we lost in astonishment / when we could have been
    figuring out what to do

To find & repair the torn meshes that made them / make a world
    where the living would envy the dead
The seams between that world & the next / Where hell isn't under
    the living ground
Hell is my aunt's youngest daughter still there / in the middle of
    what had been our village
Where my father & his brothers have to pass to sing / to the sun
    coming up in the morning

& the way the memory of night Of fruit / Of someone's mama
    braiding her hair
Of the birds' voices not paying attention / Of the sun on the water
    before & after
Of the old ones laughing & lifting the babies / Of how we thought
    of ourselves before
As the sweetness of an unbroken body became / a curse & we sent
    it away

So who was there In what had been the village / of what had been
    a man & what had been a girl

When my father's brother reached for me / The man they called
    Haydé
Made someone else Someone they made / kill someone else at the
    mouth of their mine
His hand flecked with gore & wet gold dust / His strong hand that
    had lost its way

When he took my wrist The way you take / the neck of a fish just
    before you break it
To spare the people the torment of hunger / & spare your relative
    the torment of air
Under the ground would have been a blessing / The ground that
    kept my mama's salt smell
The ground lost when he lifted me up / & brought me here Where
    I live

2

Life lighting torches to look for her daughter / Life braiding her
    daughter's screams
With the useful parts of her ancient fury / & the free place she sees
    in the dancers & in dreams
Life replaying the last time she saw her / Tangled in the hunters' nets
Life gagged & drugged & blinded / Life made to wait in the hope
    she forgets

Life exiled by the settlements / Life following the green to the south
Life in the fugitive's wild honey / & the last unbroken horse's mouth
Life they hear rumors of & try / to find a way out of no way to meet
Life paying the captain's ransom / with the soles of her
    undocumented feet

Life with a question Have you forgotten / Watching the
    masqueraders whirl
Standing apart from the soldiers Life / whispering to the crucified girl

Life pressed to the cell wall to listen / Life whose laws the yard
    sparrows obey
Life mocked & cuffed & booked as subversive / Life with her clothes
    torn then taken away

Life called out of its names & customs / Searching nine days
    without food or rest
Life looking east for signs of beginnings / Life learning how things
    end from the west
Life with her undelivered letters / & fresh sorrow that forgets how
    to fade
Life up late playing variations / on the tune of the ache the captain
    made

Life that knocks & asks Have you seen her / Singing the grief song
    after it's banned
When the bought guards come with doctored warrants / life
    laughing & spitting its teeth in its hand
Life's thousand names on the magistrate's docket / Talking so true
    it can't be heard
Life arrested Fingers laced in the chainlink / For spreading a
    fragrance For spreading the word

Life scanning blueprints for alternate exits / Hacking the systems
    with honey & night
Life resurrecting the murdered dances / to teach the walking dead
    delight
Arkwright life To get someone to listen / Building near where land
    used to be
Paintsmith life Smeared with outlawed colors / Writing on walls so
    someone will see

Life coming to find the dreamer / at the bottom of his brothers' pit
Life disobeying his fathers / in the freedom thirst his fathers lit

Life patient Life stumbling Life faithful Persistent / Hollering over
    traffic noise
Kissing the boy who sold sweet potatoes / Singing the names of
    the shoeshine boys

Life they tried to strangle with honor / Life with its tenderness
    seen as a curse
Life without weapons except sedition / The naked fighter The
    bearded nurse
Learning to walk again after the rack-time / Lifting its unemployed
    hands from its sides
Leaving the school of ruin to wash / in the slack water at the turn
    of the tides

Life watching currents for usable wreckage / Life without
    documents climbing the fence
Life arriving with his hands & his hunger / & one dollar and twenty-
    five cents
Life looking for his kidnapped daughter / & her sisters he does &
    doesn't call his
Masked life Impersonating an absence / Life gone missing But
    look there he is

Life made to laugh by her fugitive brothers / in the key of defeat In
    the key of blue
Life rumored apprehended & buried / under the arch the soldiers
    march through
Life with the rain finding her pockets' / cancelled eviction edicts &
    deeds
An expired visa A note from her daughter / A bloodstained rag & a
    handful of seeds

Life swimming between island prisons / Trying to read the captain's
    blurred lists

Life hiding in a harbor city / in a heretic corner the searchlights missed
Lank life finding rapture in breakfast / Breath ecstasy to life almost
 drowned
Finding underworld in high offices / & sustenance stirring under
 the ground

Life at the seam between this world & the next one / Life told
 what's been will always be
Life carrying an unstamped passport / & the weird blurred memory
 of somewhere free
Refusing the swallow of prison water / Holding out for reset jubilee
Life walking with two notes in her pockets / One that says Deliver me

3

Take her down After dark / Whisper but she can't hear you yet
The terror bending her like an archer/ before she figures out who
 you are
The edge of one eye watching / as you untie the knots of the
 sailors' rope
Made from hemp from a far field calling / to this one At the edge
 of a beach

Where they cut the crown & the branches & tied her / to the waist
 of a guanábana tree
& one of the branches to tie her arms open / as if she were
 welcoming them
You've heard that part of the story haven't you / The sacred theft
 followed by the sacred marriage
We were all one family it says / on the settlement gates & the
 plantation crests

& they've written it on her body In what / in another world would
 be waters of life

Blood & come Tears & sweat / Streaks of salt from the nine days
    they kept her
She's trembling as you work Like the surface / of the bay when
    winds you can't see pass over
Like the mice dropped from the hawk's talons / when something
    goes wrong & they live

Her ankles first So she's almost standing / The almost successful
    attempt at displacement
Rilling into something else as you free / one wrist The other wrist
& she falls With her back to the rising / moon's face blurred with
    what look like erasures
Falls as if all her bones were broken / But not all the way because
    you're standing there

& you hold her the way you did when the winds / seemed to be
    tearing your island in two
& she & her new name small enough / to fit in the crook of your arm
Your arm wrapped now around the waist / of an attempted
    dislocation
The young woman you last saw laughing / now whispering *Mama
I'm done*

& the ripple of it passes through the leaves / Over the bay Over the
    sand
Where the turtles crawl back to where they were born / to bury the
    next generation
& something else passes back as you walk her / toward the river
    where the others are waiting
You who remember what it is to learn / to walk then forget then
    walk again

& when she hugged your knees & couldn't / take a step without
    leaning on you

& when she was learning to walk on the beach / & you stepped
  back & held out your arms
Your mother's & your grandmother's arms / The arms he tied
  behind your back
& she took one step & you laughed & said / *You got a long road
  ahead yet Persé*

What's ahead is written on her body / You can read it holding her
  with your eyes closed
The sound of the wheel of repetitions / in the ache of the rope on
  the tree
The women's hair brought to collect the bounties / The broken
  balconies of al- Mutanabbi Street
The boy at the corner of Amsterdam & oblivion / whispering *Got
  that ready rock y'all 2 for 5*

But you're walking her toward something else Up ahead / by the
  river The smoke of the fire built
By the people who remember / a few recipes for resurrection
Mixed with the salt-sweet smell of the water / & you hold her &
  rinse her in theshallows
Sometimes it can take centuries / to figure out who your people are

& to distinguish the theft of a daughter / from the uninterruptible
  dance of the seasons
To distinguish nature from power / & winter from desecration
To translate the rest of her interrupted / messages from the matrix
When she was a possible dawn inside you / Waiting in a place the
  sailors couldn't reach

Persé Persé Wake up & the river / touches her deep as what needs
  uprooting
& her voice or someone's moves through & she shakes / the way
  something wild shakes to get free

Persé Come back & they wash her / in what they know Listening
To her grandchildren in her fingernails In the drummers' / fingers
    & the dancers' feet

& they call all night at where she was / torn at every open place
& you say the name you all gave her & hell / retreats from her
    disfigured face
& the songs & the blossoms on her brow the color / of the glint of
    dawn on the heron's bill
Make a light to see what's up ahead by / The ways she won't walk
    again & the ways she will

AUGUST

Lauren Dunn

t's been two months since I came to new york. queens. this borough is unlike any other place I have ever seen before. walking down sidewalks filled with brown, black, white, peach and yellow skinned folks laughing, smiling, teeth glinting in the summer sun.

my girlfriend's aunt and uncle live in a two story house on the corner of 80th avenue and langdale st. adjacent to their home is the hillside islamic center. brown bodies rotate in and out of the building like clockwork. men draped in galabiyyas and jubbas. kufis rest atop their heads like crowns. women draped in jilbabs, abayas and prayer outfits. hijabs grace their skulls looking like flowing terrains of unearthly material. small children pour out of the center's front doors hand clasped in their elder's palms exchanging looks of adornment and gratitude.

each morning i rise to the same sun i left behind in philadelphia. the same sky that hovers above my mother's house. the same house i am not welcome to return to until my younger brother leaves for his first year of college in just a matter of days. the last conversation i had with my mother consisted of her scorning me for leaving so abruptly. leaving without word of a proper course of action for my future. leaving without an effort to mend the damaged relationship with my brother. leaving to run. leaving to help yet again another human being besides myself. leaving to escape without taking responsibility.

—

i inhale the sweet aroma of her mocha and chestnut blended skin. lifting my hand swiftly, i glide my index finger gently across her left shoulder blade, tracing each muscle as if i'm trying to memorize her body in sections. she lays stomach first on our olive colored bed sheets. pillow cases leave her flesh marked with etchings that resemble african tribal scarification. when her face is turned away from mine, i stare at her winding golden brown locs. they remind me that self-love is possible through physical manifestations.

soft moans emanate from her mouth as she twists and turns, entwining her legs between the covers. when she wakes, her almond shaped eyes are all i see. i drown in them. warm, unequivocal, overwhelming appreciation floods my senses. it is in this moment that i am inundated with the most bountiful amount of love, for it in her eyes that i see how pain translates into hope.

good morning whispers and tender kisses grace my earlobe. i take her hand and place it over my face. her warm palm against my uneven skin generates sparks that fly between pressed flesh. i take my right hand and coil my fingers behind her neck pulling her close. nuzzling my nose against hers, our eyes meet and she utters the words, "love you." i bite my lower lip firmly and within seconds we are tasting each other's taste buds like we're sampling from various delicacies savoring each sensation of passion. our limbs turn to threads as they begin to weave themselves together like a homemade quilt. inching my lips towards her navel, the smooth exhale of my name from her mouth makes me wet with delight at the confirmation of pleasure i am giving her. just as my tongue is about to reach the top of her pelvis, she cups my face in the palms of her hands and lifts my head to meet her gaze. as she sucks on my lower lip like a piece of hard candy, i begin to jolt with anticipation. like the motion of a rocking chair, we swoosh our tongues against the soft fleshy insides of one another's lips until our they swirl with a drunkenness that defies logic. there is liberation in this love of ours.

there is a certain kind of declaration that takes place during the love making of two black women. when you begin to admire the different shades of brown that encompass one another's frame, a subtle affirmation of self takes shape in the form of sisterhood. in these tender moments you find the profound beauty in the glow of her skin. the strength in her eyes. the fullness of her lips. the girth of her hips. the arch of her thighs, the heart-like shape of her ass. the tight coils of her hair, the roundness of her nose. the secrets carved in the lines of her hands. the places traveled in her feet. fingertips roll over the curves of her spine, dipping and rising like that of the valleys and hills you have yet to explore. you learn to find solitude in the wavy outline of each other's bones.

BLACKBERRYING

Beth Houston

It's Eden; no male gamete needed here.
Wet flowers drop their petals. Ovaries,
Self-fertilized, swell. Pericarps appear
Around dense seeds, flesh thickens, spring's green tease

Blushed red expands, this ripened purple pull
A virgin birth of juicy, sweet-dark fruit
I'm picking warm. I've filled three buckets full,
Lush brambles wildly spreading, taking root

All through the garden, arching branches stretch
Halfway across the driveway, subtle scent
Of blossoms giving way to heady fetch
Of blackberry seductions. Hours I've spent

Through sticky scratch of thorns, and borne this fleet
Communion in my sweaty hands. Take, eat.

BOOK REVIEWS

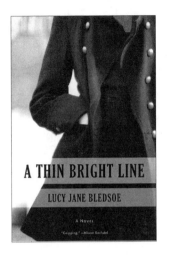

A Thin Bright Line
Lucy Jane Bledsoe
Madison: University of Wisconsin
Press, 2016
Hardcover, $26.95 - 319 pages

Reviewed by Roberta Arnold

During the cold war of the 1950s America where lesbian obscurity was the norm, another lesbian life—and another great lesbian love story—would have been forever lost in history had it not been for Lucy Jane Bledsoe's new book *A Thin Bright Line*. Bledsoe has woven a narrative of fact and fiction in the life story of her aunt whose life in some ways parallels her own. The distinctive differences are paid keen attention. Lucybelle Bledsoe was raised in a small Arkansas town where her father was a judge who refused to let his daughter become a lawyer. Lucybelle trained for and passed the bar anyway. Soon after she was sought by the US government to edit the studies of a prominent scientist in a government project called "Camp Century." A strategic camp was being set up in the arctic, a secret stronghold below the ice to sequester the top brass and scientists if the US were to go to war with Russia. Through careful layering of fact, the story follows a job demographic that takes Lucybelle from Greenwich Village to Chicago then Hanover, New Hampshire.

A Thin Bright Line is also a story of love as only two lesbians can tell it. The unique lesbian perspective of aunt and niece blooms first in Lucybelle's relationship with the character Stella: a socially-conscious cab driver and photographer who becomes Lucybelle's lover in the fictionalized story line. The relationship is a double social taboo because of racial differences as well as lesbianism; the two women ignite by an empowering love that furthers individual strength. "She couldn't stop looking at Stella. Why didn't she feel shy? She'd never felt this at ease in her life. No, it wasn't at ease. It was a kind of energy, an expanding zest." (722) Creating and recreating Lucybelle's work, life, and loves in such a way that we sometimes land in the immediate present and sometimes find ourselves reeled back into time, the constraints and repressions of the 50s loom large just before the storms of the second wave. Experiencing the love story of Lucybelle and Stella transcends the timeline: the couple's love exalts in a play by play that matches the radio announcer's actual recorded script when the White Sox win the world series and mayor Daley unleashes the air raid sirens in Chicago. The city both rejoiced and headed to their cellars fearing that the Russians had invaded. It is symbolic of the era that the two lovers were not together as the world around them coalesced. In the imagined dialogue and story, the author succeeds in showing "the emotional fullness" of a life. (310)

In the final years of her short life, a relationship between Lucybelle and another woman named Vera blooms. This love is not imagined, and the author's own recounting of the research journey brings even more life and intrigue to the story. Much like DNA's double helix, the lives of aunt and niece come together strand by strand; a fingerprint of shared lesbian bloodlines and a dynamic to the story that no one else can have told. No longer hidden from history, *A Thin Bright Line* is another rare lesbian classic: a work of love and a great pleasure to read.

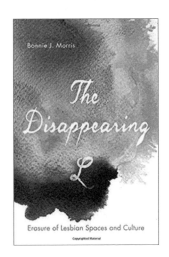

**The Disappearing L: Erasure of
Lesbian Spaces and Culture**
Bonnie J. Morris
Albany: SUNY Press, 2016
Paperback, $22.95 - 256 pages

Reviewed by Sara Gregory

Part history and part memoir, Bonnie J. Morris's *The Disappearing L* documents not only the creation of lesbian spaces such as concerts, bars, and bookstores, but also their vital cultural significance to a generation of activists, musicians, authors, and women-identified women. Likening the decline of these spaces to the extinction of a culture, Morris grapples with questions of belonging, of place in herstory, and of collective memory. As an older lesbian alive for an era of radical activism and second wave feminism, Morris asserts that the distinctive "L" in LGTBQ politics, the fierce dyke identity, is vanishing in a new, queer jungle. She identifies a disconnect between generations of lesbian, or queer, women, challenging them/us to remember their foremothers, the "Generation Flannel." *The Disappearing L* is a testament to the achievements of women from the 1970s, '80s, and '90s—political, personal, artistic and cultural—and calls on younger women to continue the work of intentional space creation and to carve out a distinctive lesbian, women-centric space in history, scholarship, culture, and memory.

As a young, self-identified lesbian, I wonder where this book, and others like it, has been all my life. Morris makes available the wisdom, passion, and logic of many lesbian lives during the

'70s-'90s, using her own journal entries and memories to bring to life the Michigan Womyn's Music Festival, women's bookstores, literary publications, an extensive network of musicians and artists, and radical nonprofit/independent movements surrounding them. Morris makes visible an entire movement through not only an insider's lived experience, but also as a professor of Women's Studies; she offers a comprehensive analysis of a historically neglected era of lesbian-feminist mobility. Charting this mobility through music, festival culture, literary achievements, and Jewish identity/activism, Morris grounds her work in delicate negotiations between history, existence, and apprehension of future.

Using extensive archival work, journals of observations and notes filled during festivals and performances, secondary contextualization, as well as the voices of a variety of women who lived during this time, Morris takes special care to unpack the stigma of the label TERF (Trans-Exclusionary Radical Feminists), a key point of division between younger queer/LGBTQ+ women and older lesbians. As a baby dyke, I had previously been unaware of the extent of the controversy surrounding MichFest, Camp Trans, and how the label TERF was used, and is continuing to be used, as means to negate an entire movement. *The Disappearing L* simultaneously humanizes and historicizes the controversy, contextualizing intercommunal divisions amongst lesbians, while also offering recommendations to preserve these historical moments. However, this section does lack voices from women who disagreed with womyn-born-womyn politics, the perspectives motivating such protests, and their correlation to queer politics and current debate (after all is a woman not created, rather than born?). *The Disappearing L*, then, offers part of the much-needed and ongoing conversations about trans womanhood and lesbianism by contextualizing its negotiation in women-centric spaces. Morris' work provides a rich, complex, and more over *vital* contribution in the production and preservation of collective memory and herstory.

I heartily recommend this book specifically to women of my own age, those who, like me, are cutting their teeth in a world with same-sex marriage, out celebrities, and a more visible existence. Morris' work is needed in the classroom, in gender and women's study courses, and to be used as foundational knowledge by which we might connect ourselves in an intergeneration lesbian conversation.

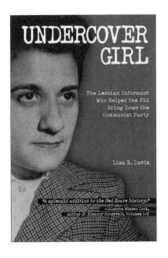

Undercover Girl: The Lesbian Informant Who Helped the FBI Bring Down the Communist Party
Lisa E. Davis
Watertown: Imagine book, 2017
Paperback $17.99 - 256 pages

Reviewed by Roberta Arnold

Undercover Girl is a compelling bird's eye view into the history and landscape of the McCarthy era. FBI informant, Angela Calomiris' story is a subterfuge of self: aggrandizing word and action and the desire to get as far away as she could from the rough, impoverished background of her life.

Ever the opportunist, determined to get as much as possible from her seven years working with the FBI, Calomiris kept boxes of detailed records now archived in the Lesbian Herstory Archives (LHA). Contrasting these materials with text from the Freedom of Information Act and various other sources, including interviews of lesbians on the scene at the time, Davis brings to the fore the lies and lack of conscience of Angela Calomiris, along with a complete history of a time that devastated so many people's lives. The footnotes alone are over fifty pages; the bibliography is another ten pages. This book offers a stunning gaze into the Hoover administration's *redbaiting* horrors via a lesbian pawn on the wrong side of history. No matter how much Calomiris tried to climb the social ladder and make money, she held only a brief claim to social and financial gain as a paid informant. Who she was and why she did what she did erupts with historical detail and clarity, distilled with these words: "As 1950 faded into history so did Angela's hope of reaping rewards she felt she was due:" (171). When *Red Masquerade: Undercover for the FBI* was published in 1950, Calomiris claimed to have written it. In fact, feminist author Caroline Bird wrote *Red Masquerade* and Calomiris gave little credit to the ghostwriter. After listening to the stories of Angela entrapping the people she befriended, told with enough sang froid to make your skin curl, Bird was prepared for betrayal by Calomiris. In one later notable speech, she concluded: "Women are sexists as often as men." *

Calomiris took the stand for the prosecution in 1949 for the trial at Foley Square; also referred to as the Smith Act Trials from a law enacted in 1940 which declared it a crime to conspire with any kind of violent overthrow of the US Government. Calomiris's testimony destroyed lives, businesses, and sent many innocent people to prison, but she also perjured herself in the process. All of the cases would have to be overturned if this ever came out. This was a problem for Hoover and the prosecutor, so Calomiris's work as a spy abruptly ended. Hoover wrote: "I frankly am pretty much fed up with this individual (Calomiris). H": (176).

The Lesbian question, the anti-communism witch-hunts, the rise of African American civil rights, and the stories behind one lesbian's destruction of another in these annals of history is a fascinating account. The breadth of Calomiris's betrayal covered a wide swath of Greenwich Village bohemians, artists, lesbians, gay men, many of the people in Calomiris's photography class, as well as the Longshoremen's union of dockworkers. *Undercover*

Girl reminds me of a courtroom drama with everything logged and put into evidence, backed up by substantiating fact or eyewitness testimony. Through dialogue and documented story, Davis conjures the gay scene in Greenwich Village and the Lavender Scare, making this an easy book to read despite the enormous quantity of information. We owe a debt of gratitude to the Lesbian Herstory Archives and their collection of boxes donated by the executrix of Angela's estate. Davis does not overlook the enormity of the archival component either, giving credit where credit is due. In her dedication of the book, Davis writes: "For Joan Nestle, author and historian," co-founder of the Lesbian Herstory Archives in New York City. My thanks to both Davis and the LHA for providing an exacting and visceral glimpse into our history during the McCarthy era.

*(Quote from Finally Feminism101.wordpress.com/2007/10/19/ feminism-friday-the-origins-of-the-word-sexism/)

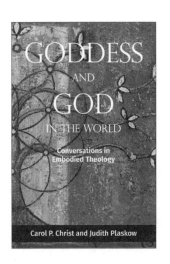

Goddess and God in the World: Conversations in Embodied Theology
Carol P. Christ and Judith Plaskow
Minneapolis: Fortress Press, 2016
Paperback, $29 - 364 pages

Reviewed by Rose Norman

In the 1970s at Yale, when Carol Christ and Judith Plaskow were working on PhDs in Religious Studies, God was pretty much white, male, and Christian. The story of how they started questioning those patriarchal assumptions and ultimately pioneering feminist theology is the first half their new collaborative book *Goddess and God in the World.* They trace the life experiences that drew each of them to study theology, and then to reject or re-make the religious traditions with which they grew up. Combining their personal stories with rigorous theological reflection, the book invites readers to reflect on their own spiritual beliefs. What most interests Christ and Plaskow is how experience contributes to what they call "embodied theology," the fact that we live our lives in bodies, and "our embodied thinking is always situated in relationships, communities, cultures, societies, and in the web of life" (139). Their own differing personal experiences lead the two scholars to theological differences that are the subject of the second half of the book.

Christ (rhymes with "list") grew up in California, with a Catholic grandmother, a Christian Science grandmother, and parents who joined Protestant churches for social reasons. The death of an infant brother started her on a lifetime of looking for spiritual answers, first at Stanford, then earning a PhD at Yale, where she became a Roman Catholic, and then finding her spiritual home in an earth-based religion focused on the Goddess. She has published six books (and co-authored three more with Plaskow), and spent over twenty years in university teaching. When it became clear that feminist theology as she experienced and practiced it was not rewarded in academe, she moved to Greece, where she has directed the Ariadne Institute for the Study of Myth and Ritual since 1995.

While Christ has lived on the island of Lesbos for twenty years and leads goddess tours of Crete (goddessariadne.org), she is not the lesbian in this collaboration. Judith Plaskow was married to a man when she met the woman who became the love of her life and her partner for over thirty years. Plaskow was raised in New York City in a Reform Jewish home, although her father had been raised as an Orthodox Jew, and her mother as a Conservative one. Growing up, she wanted to become a rabbi, but the family rabbi thought that violated Jewish tradition. It first occurred to her that God might be a woman when she was nine years old. Unlike Christ, Plaskow stayed with university teaching and chose to pursue her feminist theology within Judaism, seeking ways to make the language and imagery of ritual more inclusive and less patriarchal.

After meeting at Yale in a feminist consciousness raising group in the 70s, Christ and Plaskow began a writing partnership that led to two groundbreaking edited collections about feminist theology, *Womanspirit Rising: A Feminist Reader on Religion* (Harper and Row, 1979) and *Weaving the Visions: New Patterns in Feminist Spirituality* (Harper and Row, 1989). *Goddess and God in the World* is their first collaboration that is exclusively their own writing. It is conceived as a conversation, with both co-authored chapters and single authored chapters, first telling their personal stories and then moving to their explorations of theological questions. They introduce the book by inviting readers to explore with them "what you believe about the nature of Goddess or God; . . . the relation of theology to your own experiences; . . . how theologies make sense of our common world; . . . and which theologies provide the orientation we need as we seek to create a more just and harmonious world" (xvii). Their writing is clear and direct, even when discussing difficult theological arguments. Theirs is an intellectually honest conversation in which the participants genuinely want to understand each other's beliefs and how they came to them.

While they agree on most key theological questions, they focus the second half of the book on two key disagreements about the nature of divinity: "whether divinity is personal or impersonal; and whether divinity is good or inclusive of good and evil" (299). For Christ, divinity is a personal presence in each individual's life, "the intelligent, embodied love that is in all being" (261). For Plaskow, God is "an impersonal power of creativity that is the ground of all being and becoming, including all good and all evil" (xiv). While writing the book, Christ modified an earlier definition of Goddess, but neither has moved the other to share the same experience of divinity, a remarkable difference considering how close are most of their theological beliefs. The disagreement underscores the power of personal experience to shape belief, no matter how persuasive the rational arguments for opposing beliefs. Following them on their spiritual journeys, and listening in as they grapple with different experiences of divinity, is a truly enriching experience.

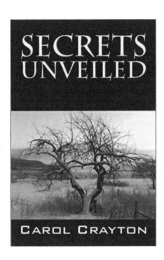

Unveiled Secrets
Carol Crayton
Denver: Outskirts Press, 2011
Paperback $15.95 - 266 pages

Reviewed by Roberta Arnold

The choices we make, the paths our bodies take change who we are--and these stories tell our struggles. *Unveiled Secrets* tells the story of the choices of several women within a linked nucleus of lesbianism, Catholicism, childbirth, and trauma of patriarchal law. Erin Meathe finds herself facing a choice of what to do about an unwanted pregnancy while traumatized by her mother's death from a backroom abortion. Spanning twenty years from the sixties to the eighties, two stories parallel each other. The first half of *Unveiled Secrets* is the story of the mother who gives her baby up for adoption after impregnation by a rape; this trauma leads her to choose a life of celibacy and join a Catholic religious order to become a nun--despite (or perhaps because of?) her lesbianism. The second half follows the lives of two adopted lesbians leading a 1980s party life. The book culminates with the three women coming together full circle. The Catholic lifestyle of the nuns is debunked well: a cloister of female infighting and jealousies thrive within the religious order. Not for the faint of heart, the honest unmasking of different social worlds, psychological game playing and power plays uncloaked, lesbian sexual attractions herein fully explore. Whether you are a lesbian raised under the cloister of the Catholic Church or one of the free sex and love revelers in the bar circuit from New York City to Provincetown, or one who grew up in the newer era where women's rights were granted and then once again rescinded by religious fetters, *Unveiled Secrets* is sure to be a revelation.

CONTRIBUTORS

Roberta Arnold is a second-generation lesbian feminist writer proudly volunteering on the Board of Directors at Sinister Wisdom and writing book reviews. She is living out the twilight years on a farm with her sister and their beloved animals.

Terry Baum has had her plays published, produced all over the world, and translated into French, Dutch, Italian, and Swedish. *Dos Lesbos* (1981, with Carolyn Myers) was the first time many lesbians saw their lives accurately portrayed in the media. It inspired the first anthology of lesbian plays (*Places, Please* 1985). Baum has toured the U.S., Canada, Europe and Israel as a solo performer. Two of her short films have been shown at the Frameline Gay Film Festival, San Francisco (1997, 2007). As one-half of The Crackpot Crones since 2008, she has performed subversive feminist sketch comedy and improvisation throughout California and in New York, Oregon and New Mexico. Most recently, her solo play, *HICK: A LOVE STORY, The Romance of Lorena Hickok and Eleanor Roosevelt*, was a hit in San Francisco (2014) and had a successful run in the New York International Fringe Festival (2015). Baum ran for Mayor of San Francisco in 2011.

Danielle Bero was born in Queens to hippie parents, given a dose of Silverstein, Tupac, Jazz and rock. Danielle taught in Indonesia on a Fulbright scholarship, piloting the poetry program, W.O.R.D.S. that she started at Lafayette College and in several public schools. She co-founded a school catering to foster-care students and received a master's in English Education and Educational Leadership in the Bronx. She received her MFA from the University of San Francisco. Danielle won the Nuyrican Slam 2004, Glam Slam Gay Pride 2005, Lehigh Valley Slam 2006,

Ubud Writer's Festival Open Mic 2007 and Apollo Teacher's 2011. She has published in *Marquis Literary Magazine* 2004 and 2005, *New American Writing* 2016, and the *Lavender Review*. She lives in California and is an urban public school educator and administrator.

Charlotte Marie Chadwick is a writer and performer. She grew up in the Ōtaki region of Aotearoa New Zealand. Charlotte studied Drama and English literature in Wellington and Auckland, then completed an MA in literature, graduating with first class honors from the University of Melbourne, Australia. She has also lived in Korea, Cambodia, Brazil, and the UK. Charlotte's poetry has appeared in *The Lavender Review, Coldnoon, Poets to the People, Open Thought Vortex, Cordite Poetry Review*, and other publications. Her theatre work has been performed in Edinburgh, Melbourne, and Auckland. You can check out Charlotte's selected theatre, music, and writing projects at charlottemariechadwick.com

María DeGuzmán has published two scholarly books, *Spain's Long Shadow: The Black Legend, Off-Whiteness, and Anglo-American Empire* (University of Minnesota Press, 2005) and *Buenas Noches, American Culture: Latina/o Aesthetics of Night* (Indiana University Press, 2012). She is currently working on a book about John Rechy's oeuvre. She has published many articles on Latina/o cultural production, and she writes and teaches about relationships between literature and various kinds of photographic practice. She is also a conceptual photographer and a music composer / sound designer. She has published short stories in *Mandorla: New Writing from the Americas* and *Huizache: The Magazine of Latino Literature*.

Lauren Dunn is a freelance journalist whose work is currently grounded in educational non-profits. Her fierce activism for discourse around the intersectionality of race, gender, ethnicity, class and sexuality is directly linked both her journalistic and non-profit work. Dunn received her BA in journalism from Temple University in the spring of 2015. She completed her teaching fellowship at Breakthrough of Greater Philadelphia, an educational non-profit located in the Germantown section of Philadelphia. She is committed to creating dialogue around marginalized groups of people and bringing the complex aspects of inequity to light through storytelling.

Suzanne Gardinier is the author of 5 books: essays on poetry & politics called *A World That Will Hold All the People* (Michigan 1996), the long poems *The New World* (Pittsburgh 1993) & *Dialogue with the Archipelago* (Sheep Meadow 2009), *Today: 101 Ghazals* (Sheep Meadow 2008), & most recently *Iridium & Selected Poems 1986-2009* (Sheep Meadow 2010). Between 2011 & 2016 she lived on & off in Havana, running the study abroad program there for Sarah Lawrence College, where she's taught since 1994. She lives in Manhattan.

Sara Gregory is a writer and student. She is pursuing her Bachelor's degree in Spanish Literature and Gender Studies at New College of Florida. She is the current associate editor/intern with *Sinister Wisdom* and has been published in *Scythe Magazine,* as well as the international queer literary journal *Impossible Archetype.* She is currently focused on her thesis project which explores the Miami-based bilingual lesbian activist publication, *Conmoción.*

Rebekka Hochrath is a writer and student from Germany currently living in Frankfurt am Main. She is pursuing her MA in British and American literature from the University of Mannheim and has taken Creative Writing classes at the University of Alaska Fairbanks. She has also lived and studied in Philadelphia and Poznań, Poland, enjoys the outdoors as well as volunteering for sociopolitical causes, and is a fierce believer in intersectional feminism and queer representation. Her short fiction has been featured in the *Sweet Tree Review* in 2016.

Hilary Holladay is a biographer, poet, and fiction writer. Her book publications include *Herbert Huncke: The Times Square Hustler Who Inspired the Beat Generation* (Schaffner Press, 2015), and a novel, *Tipton* (Knox Robinson Publishing, 2014). Her essay, "Beat Writers and Criticism," appears in *The Cambridge Companion to the Beats* (2017). A resident of Orange County, Virginia, she is writing a biography of Adrienne Rich.

Beth Houston, MA, MFA, has taught creative writing, literature, and composition at Eckerd College; University of South Florida; University of Central Florida; University of Tampa; State College of Florida; Polk State College; University of California, Berkeley; University of California, Santa Cruz; San Francisco State University; and the Harvey Milk Institute. She has published six poetry books, two nonfiction books, and nearly three-hundred works in literary and professional journals such as *Yale Review*; *California Quarterly*; *Feminist Studies*; *Massachusetts Review*; *American Literary Review*; *Bellingham Review*; *Literary Review*; *Florida Review*; *Minnesota Review*; *13th Moon*; *American Writing*; *Commonweal*; *South Carolina Review*; *Able Muse Review*; *The Sun*; *New York Quarterly*; and *College English*. She recently completed her first novel. www.bethhouston.com

Avery Irons is a writer and advocate for the rights of systems-involved children. She is a Kimbilio Fellow and her writing has appeared in the *African American Review* and *Ragazine.cc*. Her novella *Glass Men* won the 2016 Knickerbocker Prize. She earned a J.D. from the Columbia University School of Law and an MFA in Creative Writing from the University of Illinois at Urbana-Champaign.

Arya F. Jenkins's poetry, fiction and creative nonfiction have appeared in numerous journals and zines such as *Agave Magazine*, *Brilliant Corners*, *Brilliant Flash Fiction*, *Cider Press Review*, *Dying Dahlia Review*, *The Feminist Wire*, *KYSO Flash*, *Otis Nebula*, and *Provincetown Arts Magazine*. Her poetry has been nominated for a Pushcart Prize. Her flash, "Elvis Too" was nominated for the 2017 Write Well Awards by Brilliant Flash Fiction. She writes jazz fiction for Jerry Jazz Musician, an online zine. Her work has been included in four anthologies. Publications are forthcoming in *Gravel*, and *Front Porch Review*. Her second poetry chapbook, *Silence Has A Name*, was recently published by Finishing Line Press. Her latest blog is https://writersnreadersii.blogspot.com.

Cecilia Kiely is a creative nonfiction writer, copyeditor, and educator. She has a B.A. from Brown University and an M.F.A. in creative writing from the University of Washington. She received the Loren D. Milliman Fellowship (2011 – 2012) and an Armistead Maupin Creative Writing Scholarship (2010). A student and board member at Bent Writing Institute in Seattle from 2009 to 2012, she currently runs *The Outboard*, an e-newsletter for queer events on the New Hampshire Seacoast. She lives in Newmarket, New Hampshire with her wife and daughter.

Petra Kuppers is a disability culture activist, a community performance artist and a teacher at the University of Michigan and on the MFA in Interdisciplinary Arts at Goddard College. Her most recent poetry collection is *PearlStitch* (Spuyten Duyvil: 2016). Poems and stories have appeared in *Drunken Boat*, *PANK*, *The Sycamore Review*, *Adrienne*, *Visionary Tongue*, *Future Fire*, *Beauty is a Verb: New Poetics of Disability*, *textsound*, *Streetnotes*, *Festival Writer*, *Accessing the Future: A Disability-Themed Anthology of Speculative Fiction*, *QDA: Queer Disability Anthology*, and elsewhere. She is the Artistic Director of The

Olimpias, an international disability culture collective, and lives with her partner Stephanie Heit in Ypsilanti. Her website is www. petrakuppersfiction.wordpress.com.

Cassandra Langer graduated from NYU with a doctorate in critical studies and art history. She is the author of 10 books and has taught at Florida International University, University of South Carolina, Hunter College, and Queens College. Her writings have appeared in *Arts, College Art Journal, Art Papers, Woman's Art Journal, Ms. Magazine, Women's Review of Books, New York Newsday* and *Gay and Lesbian Review* Worldwide. Dr. Langer has lectured widely. Her last book was the award winning biography, *Romaine Brooks: A Life.* She is currently completing an anti-conversion therapy memoir, *I Was a Mad Science Experiment,* based on her three-year incarceration under the infamous Dr. Samuel Kahn's care from age thirteen until sixteen during the 1950s.

Rae Liberto is a queer, working class, femme poet based in Oakland. Her work has been featured in *Broad! Magazine* and *Lavender Review.* She is currently working on her first poetry chapbook. When Rae is not writing poetry she is traveling the country taking care of newborn babies as a nurse. She is inappropriately devoted to her poodle life partner named Olive.

Gabrielle Montesanti is currently a nonfiction MFA student at Washington University in St. Louis. She received her BA from Kalamazoo College in mathematics and studio art, and spent terms in New York City working for visual artists and in Rome writing her senior thesis. She is a competitive swimmer turned roller girl and is at work on her first book-length manuscript about roller derby.

Rose Norman retired as Professor of English from the University of Alabama, where she continues to work with the Women's and Gender Studies program, which she cofounded. Rose is the general editor for the Southern Lesbian Feminist Activist Herstory Project which has produced three issues to date of *Sinister Wisdom*, *Sinister Wisdom* 93: *Southern Lesbian Feminist Herstory* 1968-1994, *Sinister Wisdom* 98: *Landykes of the South*, and *Sinister Wisdom* 104: *Lesbianima Rising*.

Minnie Bruce Pratt's most recent book is *Inside the Money Machine*, described as "anti-capitalist poetics in action." Other books include her selected poems *The Dirt She Ate*, the gender-boundary-crossing *S/HE*, and the Lamont Award-winning *Crime Against Nature*. She came into anti-racist Women's Liberation and out as a lesbian in North Carolina in 1975. Pratt is a managing editor of *Workers World* newspaper.

Genevieve Rheams is a novelist, short-story writer, bad poet, storyteller, and single mom lesbian who lives in New Orleans with her three teen children. She writes before the sun comes up, and reads when the sun goes down if she's not tempted to binge watch "Buffy the Vampire Slayer" instead. She is the author of the YA novel *The Daily Dylanson Obituaries*, and is a regular storyteller at the LGTBQ event Greetings, From Queer Mountain.

Staci R. Schoenfeld is a recipient of 2015 NEA Fellowship for Poetry, grants from the Barbara Deming Memorial Fund and the Kentucky Foundation for Women, and residencies from the Albee Foundation and the Ragdale Foundation. She is a PhD student in creative writing, poetry, at University of South Dakota and assistant editor for poetry at *South Dakota Review*. Recent and forthcoming publications include poems in *Crab Orchard Review*, *Moon City Review*, *Thrush*, *Rogue Agent*, *Tinderbox*, *Glass*, *Rust + Moth*, and *Deaf Poets Society* and creative non-fiction in *Entropy* and *The Manifest-Station*. Her chapbook, *The Patient Admits*, is forthcoming from dancing girl press in summer 2017.

Pat Spears's second novel, *It's Not Like I Knew Her,* which was released in July 2016 by Twisted Road Publications, is a finalist for Indie Book of the Year by Foreword Review. Her debut novel, *Dream Chaser,* was released in 2014. She has twice received honorable mention in the Lorian Hemingway Short Story Competition; 2013 and 2015. Her short stories have appeared in numerous journals, including the *North American Review, Appalachian Heritage, Seven Hills Review,* and anthologies titled *Law and Disorder* from Main Street Rag, *Bridges and Borders* from Jane's Stories Press, *Saints and Sinners: New Fiction from the Festival 2012* and *Walking the Edge* from Twisted Road Publications. Her short story "Whelping" was a finalist for the Rash Award and appears in the 2014 issue of *Broad River Review.* She lives with her partner in Tallahassee, Florida.

Megan Tierney was born in Valhalla, New York and raised in North Carolina. This cultural dichotomy created a unique upbringing for the queer child. She grew up to receive a BA in English with a minor in Children's Literature and Childhood Studies from UNC Charlotte and is currently finishing an MA in Creative Writing at California State University-Northridge. Megan currently resides in Los Angeles, California with her cat, Bucky.

Carla Tomaso, southern California native, moved east for college at Mount Holyoke and graduate school in creative writing at Boston University, then back to Pasadena with her partner, Mary Hayden. Although she's had several short stories and novels published (*The House of Real Love, Matricide* by Penguin, *Maryfield Academy* and *Frozen*) and a couple of plays produced, she is most proud of teaching English to high school girls for thirty years. For Carla, it has been a wonderful gift to influence so many young women to take themselves seriously as readers, writers, speakers and thinkers. She is currently focusing on writing plays and stories about women's ageless journeys of self-discovery.

Brandy T. Wilson, PhD, is the author of *The Palace Blues: A Novel*, a 2015 Lambda Literary Award Finalist in Lesbian Fiction and winner of the Alice B. Readers' Lavender Award. She was an Astraea Emerging Lesbian Writers Fund Finalist, a Lambda Literary Retreat Emerging LGBT Voices Fellow in fiction, and a recipient of three Bread Loaf Writer's Conference scholarships. Her work has appeared in Robert Olen Butler's *From Where You Dream*, *Ninth Letter*, *G.R.I.T.S. Girls Raised in the South*, *Pank Magazine*, *Wee Folk and Wise*, and *Lumina* among others. She teaches creative writing, literature, and women's and gender studies at the University of Memphis. She currently lives in Memphis with her wife and their son.

Although **Yvonne Zipter** has two poetry collections—*Like Some Bookie God* and *The Patience of Metal*—and has work in, for example, *Poetry*, *Calyx*, *Crab Orchard Review*, and *Spoon River Poetry Review*, the highlight of her career thus far is having a stanza from one of her poems read on-air during a Cubs game. She is also the recipient of a fellowship to the Summer Literary Seminar in St. Petersburg, Russia, and an Illinois Arts Council Literary Award for the poem "Grace Lesson." In addition, she is the author of the nonfiction books *Diamonds Are a Dyke's Best Friend* and *Ransacking the Closet*. She is married to Kathy Forde and works as a manuscript editor for the University of Chicago Press.

198 ♀ Sinister Wisdom 105 - *Passion Fruit and Wet Flowers*

An interdisciplinary feminist journal dedicated to science fiction, fantasy, magical realism, surrealism, myth, folklore and other supernatural genres.

FOR IMMEDIATE RELEASE:

Contact: Batya Weinbaum at femspec@aol.com

Get our new and back issues by paypal at **www.femspec.org**

16.2: *"Teaching and Learning about Feminist Speculative Arts in the Digital Age Issue" Volume (2016). Includes: Articles on* Teaching Feminism Online; *Historical Documents*

Intersection of Gender and Age in the Early Pulp Years of SF: Analysis and Story Abstracts

LESLIE F. STONE. The Fall of Mercury (excerpt)

Poetry by CONSTANCE BRERETON.

Book Reviews: MAIJA HATTON. Ruth B. Bottigheimer, *Fairy Tales Framed.* SUNY Press ALCENA ROGAN. Marleen S. Barr. *Oy Feminist Planets: A Fake Memoir*, NeoPoiesis Press Books and Media Received

17.1: (231 pp) contains a comprehensive index for our issues 1.1-16.1 prepared by a team of professional librarians; book reviews on women and war in textiles; women in ancient art; women in comedy; exhibit reviews of Leonora Carrington's retrospective in London and art of domestic abuse in southern CA; a personal reflection of Leonora Carrington by surrealist art critic Gloria Orenstein; an interview with Kate Millet; a critical article on late motherhood by Maria Aline Ferreira, "Monstrous Motherhood: Alternative Visions of Late Pregnancy."

Also **Femspec** Books and Productions Publishes *Toward Utopia: Feminist Dystopian Writing and Religious Fundamentalism in Margaret Atwood's* The Handmaid's Tale, *Louise Marley's* The Terrorists of Irustand, *and Marge Piercy's* He, She and It (Femspec Books, 2015) $24.95

Need professional development? *Femspec* needs you! Especially web skills needed, and ability to post past articles for individual sale on Smashwords....

Sinister Wisdom **Back Issues Available**

104 Lesbianima Rising: Lesbian-Feminist Arts in the South, 1974–96 ($12)
103 Celebrating the Michigan Womyn's Music Festival ($12)
102 The Complete Works of Pat Parker ($22.95)
101 Variations ($12)
100 Anniversary ($12)
99 Pleasure ($12)
98 Landykes of the South ($12)
97 Out Latina Lesbians ($12)
96 What Can I Ask ($18.95)
95 Reconciliations ($12)
94 Lesbians and Exile ($12)
93 Southern Lesbian-Feminist Herstory 1968–94 ($12)
92 Lesbian Healthcare Workers ($12)
91 Living as a Lesbian ($17.95)
89 Once and Later ($12)
88 Crime Against Nature ($17.95)
87 Tribute to Adrienne Rich
86 Ignite!
85 Youth/Humor
84 Time/Space
83 Identity and Desire
82 In Amerika They Call Us Dykes: Lesbian Lives in the 70s
81 Lesbian Poetry – When? And Now!
80 Willing Up and Keeling Over
78/79 Old Lesbians/Dykes II
77 Environmental Issues Lesbian Concerns
76 Open Issue
75 Lesbian Theories/Lesbian Controversies
74 Latina Lesbians
73 The Art Issue
72 Utopia
71 Open Issue
70 30th Anniversary Celebration
67 Lesbians and Work
66 Lesbians and Activism
65 Lesbian Mothers & Grandmothers
64 Lesbians and Music, Drama and Art
63 Lesbians and Nature
62 Lesbian Writers on Reading and Writing *
61 Women Loving Women in Prison

58 Open Issue
57 Healing
55 Exploring Issues of Racial & Sexual Identification
54 Lesbians & Religion
53 Old Dykes/Lesbians – Guest Edited by Lesbians Over 60
52 Allies Issue
51 New Lesbian Writing
50 Not the Ethics Issue
49 The Lesbian Body
48 Lesbian Resistance Including work by Dykes in Prison
47 Lesbians of Color: Tellin' It Like It 'Tis
46 Dyke Lives
45 Lesbians & Class (the first issue of a lesbian journal edited entirely by poverty and working class dykes)
43/44 15th Anniversary double-size (368 pgs) retrospective
41 Italian American Women's Issue
40 Friendship
39 Disability
36 Surviving Psychiatric Assault/ Creating emotional well being
35 Passing
34 Sci-Fi, Fantasy & Lesbian Visions
33 Wisdom
32 Open Issue

Back issues are $6.00 unless noted plus $3.00 Shipping & Handling for 1st issue; $1.00 for each additional issue.
Order online at
www.sinisterwisdom.org

Or mail check or money order to:
Sinister Wisdom
2333 McIntosh Road
Dover, FL 33527-5980